Lernkrimi Englisch

Last Exit Waterloo Bridge

Bernie Martin
Sarah Trenker

compact

Weitere Informationen zu Compact Lernkrimis finden Sie am Ende des Buches und unter www.lernkrimi.de.

Baierbrunner Straße 27, 81379 München
Ausgabe 2017

Redaktion: Helga Aichele
Fachkorrektur: Alison Frankland
Produktion: Ute Hausleiter
Titelillustration: Karl Knospe
Lernkrimi-Logo: Carsten Abelbeck
Gestaltung: EKH Werbeagentur GbR, textum GmbH
Umschlaggestaltung: red.sign GbR, Stuttgart; Hartmut Baier

ISBN 978-3-8174-1863-3
381741863/1

www.compactverlag.de, www.lernkrimi.de, www.facebook.com/lernkrimi

Vorwort

Liebe Leserin, lieber Leser,

sicher zum Lernerfolg – mit Spaß und Spannung! Die Compact Lernkrimis mit ihrer Kombination aus Lektüre und didaktischem Übungsanteil eignen sich hervorragend, um breite Sprachkompetenzen in der Fremdsprache zu erwerben. Der Lernende wird dabei durch die spannende Handlung, das angemessene Sprachniveau und den stetig ansteigenden Schwierigkeitsgrad der Übungen gefördert und motiviert.
Entwickelt nach neuesten Erkenntnissen der Fremdsprachendidaktik, sind Compact Lernkrimis das ideale Medium für einen Lernerfolg im Selbststudium. Durch die kleinen Texteinheiten und den hohen Übungsanteil sind sie aber auch als Unterrichtslektüre bestens geeignet.

So lernen Sie mit Compact Lernkrimis:

- **Mit Begeisterung lernen:** Die packende Krimihandlung motiviert Sie beim Lesen des englischen Originaltextes.
- **Wissen intensivieren und erweitern:** Durch die Kombination aus didaktisch aufbereiteter Lektüre und textbezogenen Übungen testen und trainieren Sie Ihre Sprachkenntnisse effektiv. Vokabelangaben auf jeder Seite unterstützen Sie beim Lesen.
- **Systematisch lernen:** Knüpfen Sie an Ihr individuelles Sprachniveau an und setzen Sie eigene Lernziele.
- **Unabhängig sein:** Lernen Sie individuell – wo und wann immer Sie wollen.

Viel Spaß beim spannenden Erlernen der englischen Sprache
wünscht Ihnen

Prof. Dr. Christiane Neveling
Didaktik der romanischen Sprachen, Universität Leipzig

Inhalt

Terminus Waterloo Bridge

Bernie Martin

1 The Killer

Nobody knows his real name. The professional killer known as "Marco" sits in a jet on his way from Rome to London and thinks about his mission. He spent the last few years getting revenge on the people who killed his family. Now there is only one person left on his list and that person is in London.
Marco closes his eyes and falls into a troubled sleep.
Once again he sees himself as a small boy: he is getting water for his family from the stream. Then he hears the scream of the rockets that are flying over his head, racing towards his village. The sound of the rockets is still very clear to him and he jumps in his sleep.
His body jerks in his seat as he relives the explosions and the terrible screams of the villagers. He runs to his home in shock, whispering the name of his parents and his little sister, Jasmin. The first thing he notices is the smell of burnt flesh, the flesh of people, then he sees what is left of his home. The hot, bitter tears come and he runs to the living area of his home. He sees his father first. The old Enfield rifle is still warm

terminus	Endstation
revenge	Rache
stream	Bach
rocket	Rakete
to jump	*hier*: zusammenzucken
to jerk	zucken
to relive sth.	etw. nochmals durchleben
villager	Dorfbewohner(in)
to whisper	flüstern
rifle	Gewehr

in his father's hand. He shot at the jets.
Marco shakes his head at his father's courage. Marco closes his father's eyes and lets out a great scream of pain. His scream is suddenly cut off when he sees his mother's sandal sticking out of the remains of their house. He crawls across the stones and sees that his mother died because she was trying to protect her daughter, Jasmin. Marco gently rolls his mother's body off his sister, lifts her in his arms and carries her to the foot of a tree where there is shade.

remains *pl*	Überreste
to crawl	kriechen
to protect	(be)schützen
gently	sanft, zärtlich
yard	Längenmaß: 91 cm
to squeeze	drücken
sigh	Seufzer
prayer	Gebet

Jasmin wants water and Marco looks around for the water bucket. It is only twenty yards away, but Marco can't remember carrying it that far. He jumps up and collects the bucket as fast as he can. He places the bucket next to Jasmin and bends down to lift her head so that she can drink.
"Marco. I'm cold."
Marco panics[i] because it is a very hot day.
"It's okay, Jasmin. I'm here."
"Marco. Why is it getting dark so early? I don't understand."
Jasmin squeezes Marco's hand, gives one last sigh and dies in his arms.

Bei der Verlaufsform und dem Partizip des englischen Verbs **to panic** *(in Panik geraten, durchdrehen)* wird aus dem **c** ein **ck:**

He panics.	Er gerät in Panik.
He's panicking.	Er dreht durch.
She panicked.	Sie geriet in Panik.

"Jasmin! Don't go! You can't leave me alone. Come back, Jasmin. Please, come back."
Tears stream down Marco's face. He lays his sister down with great care, not wanting to hurt her. He cries a few prayers for her soul and then stands up. He angrily shakes his fist at the sky and screams: "I will have my revenge!"

Exercise 1: Multiple choice. Welche Übersetzung stimmt? Kreuzen Sie an!

1. Marco, mir ist kalt.
   a) ☒ Marco. I am cold.
   b) ☐ Marco. I am a cold person.

2. Er sieht seinen Vater zuerst.
   a) ☐ His father sees him first.
   b) ☒ He sees his father first.

3. Marco schüttelt seinen Kopf.
   a) ☒ Marco shakes his head.
   b) ☐ Marco nods his head.

4. Ich verstehe nicht.
   a) ☐ I understand not.
   b) ☒ I don't understand.

5. Du kannst mich nicht alleine lassen.
   a) ☐ You should leave me alone.
   b) ☒ You can't leave me alone.

"Would you like something to drink before we land, sir?" Marco wakes up to see a pretty stewardess smile at him. "No thank you. I'm fine."

"We'll land at Heathrow in about ten minutes, sir. Could you please fasten your seat belt?"
Marco smiles, nods and fastens his seat belt. He is still sweating from his dream. His last thought before he lands is: When this last person is dead and my family is revenged, maybe then I can dream the dreams of a child again.

Thirty minutes later, Ali is waiting for Marco in the arrivals area. He will meet Marco for the first time. He only knows the legend.
Marco is his hero. He looks for a man in a beige suit, with a black carnation pinned to the jacket. This is the agreed recognition signal and Ali is very excited. Then he sees him and his heart misses a beat.
Marco is a handsome man with short black hair. Ali waves and the man smiles, showing very white teeth.

to nod	nicken
carnation	Nelke
recognition signal	Erkennungszeichen
to wave (one's hands)	winken
to approach	sich nähern
shiver	Schauer, Zittern
deadliness	Tödlichkeit
to grab	packen, greifen
safe house	sicherer Unterschlupf
arms dealer	Waffenhändler

As Marco approaches, Ali sees that his eyes are completely black. A little shiver of fear goes through Ali when he realizes that the smile on the mouth is in complete contrast to the deadliness of the eyes.
He grabs Marco's hands. "Greetings, Master!"
"Hello, Ali. You weren't followed, were you?"
"No, Master. I have the car waiting. I'll drive you to the safe house."
Marco nods. "The arms dealer?"
"He is expecting you, Master. Should I drive you there now?"
"No. Tomorrow will be soon enough."

Exercise 2: Odd one out. **Welches Wort passt nicht in die Reihe? Unterstreichen Sie das „schwarze Schaf"!**

1. see sea saw seen
2. jacket trousers coat anorak
3. boys childs girls children
4. eyes feet nose mouth
5. handsome slim beautiful pretty
6. car lorry truck motorbike

The next day, Ali drives Marco to the arms dealer in Soho. Marco tells Ali to wait in the car with the engine running.
Marco enters the newsagent's shop and locks the door behind him. There is a fat man behind the counter. He has dark, greasy hair and is very nervous. He looks at Marco with fear in his eyes and says, "Good morning. Can I help you?"
"It is very cold in London today."
The fat man recognizes the code. "You want to buy weapons?"
"Yes."
"Follow me."
The fat man goes to a room at the back of the shop. He pushes a table and carpet aside. There is a door in the floor and he lifts it. Marco sees steps to the cellar and he follows the fat man down. The room is full of weapons. Marco picks up a gun and looks at it. He can see that the fat man is still afraid.
"Why are you so nervous?"
"Just tell me what you want and leave."

engine	Motor
newsagent	Zeitungshändler, Zeitschriften-laden
counter	Tresen, Theke
greasy	fettig
ammunition	Munition
bookshelves *pl*	Bücherregale
to dial	wählen (Telefon)
prison	Gefängnis

"You aren't very polite, Mr...?"
"No names. Now, what do you want to buy?"
Marco chooses some weapons and asks the fat man the price.
"Ten thousand pounds."
"Too expensive. I'll give you five thousand."
"I have to live, you know. I'll take seven thousand and give you ten boxes of ammunition."
Marco agrees and pays cash. The fat man's hands shake as he packs the guns in brown paper. Marco takes the packages and goes up the stairs. He walks to the shop door and unlocks it. He opens the door and Ali gets out of the car. Marco gives him the packages and whispers, "Drive round the block."
Ali nods. Marco goes back into the shop, closes the door and hides behind some bookshelves. A few minutes later he hears the fat man close the door to the cellar. The fat man then hurries to the shop door, nervously looks out and locks the door. Then he goes to the phone on the counter and dials a number.
"Hello. Is that the police?"
"Yes, sir. How can I help you?"
"Shut up and listen. I want to speak to Inspector Fletcher. We have a deal."
"Could you give me your name, please?"
"Tell Fletcher that Adam Giles phoned. She promised I wouldn't go to prison. Someone just bought two rifles and two handguns from me."
Marco quietly moves towards the counter.
"Mr Giles, could you give me your address, sir?"
"Yes. It's... Aargh!"

piano wire	Klavierdraht
pedestrian	Fußgänger(in)

Marco doesn't want anyone to hear the sound of a gun, so he pulls the piano wire tight around the fat man's neck. He lowers the body to the floor behind the counter. He quickly looks out of the window to check if people on the busy street have noticed anything. But the pedestrians just walk on. Good. Marco goes to the door and waves to Ali at the end of the street. Marco jumps in the car and they drive off.

The telephone is still swinging in the air. A voice can be heard.

"Mr Giles! Are you still there? Is something wrong?"

Exercise 3: Translation. Übersetzen Sie die folgenden Aussagen!

1. Ich möchte Inspector Fletcher sprechen.

   ____

2. Sie sind nicht sehr höflich.

   ____

3. Guten Morgen, kann ich Ihnen helfen?

   ____

4. Warum sind Sie so nervös?

   ____

5. Ali steigt aus dem Auto aus.

   ____

6. Er geht zur Ladentür und schließt sie auf.

   ____

2 Fletcher and Walsh

A short time later, Inspector Roberta Fletcher of the Metropolitan Police is sitting at her desk. There is a knock at the door.

"Come in."

Roberta's assistant Jack Walsh enters the room. Roberta looks at him and sees a very fit man in his thirties, who goes to a fitness club every day of the year. He has bright red hair and wears glasses with thick black frames. Jack is a **confirmed bachelor**. He still lives with his mother in Wembley and loves **researching murder cases** from the nineteenth century. Roberta smiles at his **tweed** suit and colourful **dickie bow**.

"Jack, I'll have to take you shopping for clothes. You look like a very boring English professor."

Jack **stares** into her brown eyes.

"Yes, Roberta. You say that at least once a week."

Jack is interrupted by Roberta's telephone. She picks it up.

"Inspector Fletcher here?"

"Hello, Inspector. This is **Constable** Foster. I **received** a call from a Mr Adam Giles a few minutes ago. He asked for you by name."

confirmed bachelor	überzeugter Junggeselle
to research	(er)forschen
murder	Mord
case	*hier*: Fall; Koffer
tweed	Wollstoff, Tweed
dickie bow	Fliege (Krawatte)
to stare	starren
constable	Polizist, Wachtmeister
to receive	erhalten; empfangen

choking noises *pl*	Würgegeräusche
bell	Klingel, Glocke
receiver	Telefonhörer; Empfänger

"I know Mr Giles, Constable. What does he want?"
"Well, that's the strange thing, Inspector. He seemed to be cut off, but I could hear choking noises in the background."
Roberta starts taking notes. "Did he give you his address?"
"No, but I have it here on my computer screen."
"Okay. Give it to me please."
"It's Adam Giles, 38 Frith Street, a newsagent's in Soho."
"Right, thanks. We're on our way."
Roberta tells Jack what the phone call was about and they leave the office quickly.

Exercise 4: True or false? Welche der folgenden Aussagen sind wahr? Kreuzen Sie an!

1. Marco is from Italy. ❒
2. Jack is Roberta's assistant. ❒
3. Roberta is an inspector. ❒
4. Adam Giles is very handsome. ❒
5. Jack hates sport. ❒
6. Jack has short, blond hair. ❒

They arrive fifteen minutes later. Roberta tries the shop door and it opens. As she puts her foot on the doormat, a bell starts ringing at the back of the shop. Jack follows Roberta in and both look around the shop. Roberta hears a strange noise and walks to the counter. She sees the telephone, but the receiver is hanging somewhere behind the counter. She leans over the counter and catches her breath.

"Jack!"

"Be patient, Roberta. I haven't found anything yet."

Roberta shouts, "Jack! I've found a body. I think it's Giles."

Jack runs behind the counter.

"You're right, Roberta. It's Giles. He's dead. Look, you call for back-up and I'll stay here with the body."

to catch one's breath	den Atem anhalten
back-up	Verstärkung
emergency service	Notdienst
I'm afraid (not)	leider (nicht)
crime scene	Tatort
Oh dear!	Meine Güte!; Oje!
to arrest	verhaften

Roberta walks to the door and calls the emergency services on her mobile phone. Just as she hangs up, an old woman tries to enter the shop and Roberta blocks her way.

"I'm sorry Madam, but you can't come in here."

"Why not? The sign says 'open' and I need to buy a newspaper."

"I'm afraid that's not possible, Madam. This shop is now a crime scene."

The old lady puts her hand to her mouth. "Oh dear! What happened then?"

"Erm... There was an accident, Madam. Could you please leave now?"

"Oh, all right. You should be out arresting those dangerous drivers. One left this shop half an hour ago and nearly ran me down. Goodbye."

It takes a few seconds for Roberta to understand what the old woman is saying.

"One moment please, Madam. Could you say that again, please?"

"First you want me to leave and now you want me to stay. You young people don't know what you want."

"Yes. You're right, Madam. Now, could you please repeat what you said?"

"I said: I need to buy a newspaper."
"I don't mean that, Madam. Would you please repeat what you said after that?"

Exercise 5: Opposites. Lesen Sie weiter und tragen Sie das Gegenteil der angegebenen Wörter ein!

"Well. Half an hour ago I was crossing the **zebra crossing** about a hundred yards up the street. I saw a car stop **1.** inside ______________ the shop and a man got **2.** out ______________. Then the driver just raced along the street and nearly knocked me **3.** up __________. He didn't even brake, the hooligan."

"I see, Madam. Did it really take you half an hour to **4.** run ______________ a hundred yards to the shop?"

The **5.** young ______________ lady's face reddens.

"Well, I saw Mrs Dowd in her garden, so I had to tell her about my escape from **6.** life ______________."

"I understand, Madam. Can you describe the car or the two **7.** women ______________, please?"

"The car is **8.** black ______________ and quite small. I'm not usually **9.** bad ______________ at **makes**, but it looks the same as my **nephew's**. German, I think. Something to do with sport."

"Do you mean 'Golf', Madam?" Roberta asks.
"Yes. That's it."
"What about the men, Madam. Can you describe them for me?" she asks the old lady.
"Not really. They both have dark hair and aren't pale enough to be Englishmen. I would say Italian or Greek."
"And do you perhaps remember the registration number of the car, Madam?"
"No. My eyes are not as good as they used to be. Although I remember a 'B' registration. That's the same as my nephew's car, but his is red."
"Well. Thank you very much, Madam. Your information helps me a lot."

zebra crossing	Zebrastreifen
make	Marke, Fabrikat
nephew	Neffe
pale	blass, bleich
registration number	polizeiliches Kennzeichen
used to be	(mal) gewesen sein
nowadays	heutzutage
to disturb	*hier*: durcheinanderbringen
evidence	Beweis(e)
storeroom	Lagerraum
kitchenette	Kochnische
disgust	Ekel

"You're welcome," the old lady replies. "You are a very nice girl. Pretty, too, and so polite. I don't meet many of those nowadays. Goodbye, my dear."
Roberta turns and smiles. It's nice to be called a girl again, she thinks.
While Roberta is talking to the woman, Jack is looking around the shop. He is very careful not to disturb any evidence. He finds nothing in the shop, though, and goes through to the back room. It is used as a storeroom and has a little kitchenette. Dirty dishes with left-over food are lying in the sink and Jack holds his nose in disgust.
He turns and looks slowly around the room. The first thing he notices is that the table and chairs aren't straight. He's not surprised,

tidy	ordentlich, aufgeräumt
handle	Griff; (Tür-)Klinke
to whistle	pfeifen
trapdoor	Falltür
switch	Schalter
mounted on	montiert auf
handrail	Handlauf
amazement	Erstaunen
neat	ordentlich
gadget	Gerät, technische Spielerei
kind	Art, Sorte

because Mr Giles wasn't a very tidy person. Then he sees that a corner of the carpet is folded over.

Jack bends down to straighten it and discovers a handle built into the wooden floor. He whistles and pulls the carpet all the way back. There is a trapdoor set into the floor.

He grabs the handle and pulls the trapdoor open. There are steps leading down into the darkness. Jack sees a switch mounted on the handrail and pushes it down.

Suddenly there is light and Jack goes down a few steps. His mouth opens in amazement. The room is neat, clean and organized. The shelves on all four walls are full of weapons and gadgets of every kind. Jack quickly goes back up the steps and goes outside to look for Roberta.

Police cars are now arriving at the shop, and Roberta shows them where to find the body. She is writing down what the[i] old lady said, when Jack comes out of the shop. She tells Jack about the old lady and Jack tells her about his discovery. Then they go back into the newsagent's, where Jack shows Roberta where he found the weapons.

Together, they have another look around the shop, to see if they

> Achtung Aussprache:
>
> Wenn der Artikel **the** vor einem Vokal steht, wird das **e** wie **i** gesprochen. Bei **the lady** hört man also ein **e,** bei **the old lady** ein **i.**
>
> the lady [ðə'leɪdi]
>
> the old lady [ðiəʊld'leɪdi]

can find any helpful clues. However, they find nothing of interest.
Then the shop is full of people. A doctor is examining Mr Giles as a grey-haired man approaches Roberta and Jack.
"Hello, Inspector Fletcher. Didn't we work together on the murder in the docks last year?" he asks.
"Yes we did, Mr Harris. How are you?"

clue	Hinweis, Spur
docks *pl*	Hafen(anlage)
forensics	Spurensicherung
to trace	aufspüren; (zurück) verfolgen
file	Akte; Datei
to involve	beteiligen
criminal record	Vorstrafe; Vorstrafenregister

"I'm fine thanks, Inspector." He looks at Jack.
"I'm sorry, Mr Harris. This is Jack Walsh, my assistant," Roberta explains.
"I'm pleased to meet you, Mr Walsh," the forensics expert replies. "Right, we need to start collecting evidence, so I'm afraid I will have to ask you to leave now."
"We understand, Mr Harris. Goodbye then."
Mr Harris waves his hand at them as he opens his case full of instruments.
Roberta and Jack decide to go back to the office and try and trace the car.

Jack tells Roberta that there are thousands of white Golfs registered in London, but only 84 have a "B" registration. Jack prints the 84 registration numbers out and gives Roberta half of them. After ten minutes, Roberta leans back in her chair.
"This isn't getting us anywhere, Jack. Can you think of anything else we could try?"
"I have an idea. Why don't we run the 84 names through our criminal files? There's a pretty good chance that whoever is involved has a criminal record."
"Good idea, Jack! Let's do that."

Exercise 6: Multiple choice. Wählen Sie die richtige Variante aus!

1. Roberta is a very ______________ girl.
   a) ❒ bad
   b) ❒ angry
   c) ❒ nice

2. The table and chairs aren't ______________.
   a) ❒ wood
   b) ❒ straight
   c) ❒ metal

3. This is Jack, my ______________.
   a) ❒ husband
   b) ❒ boyfriend
   c) ❒ assistant

4. I am ______________ to meet you.
   a) ❒ pleased
   b) ❒ lucky
   c) ❒ angry

5. Mr Giles wasn't a very ______________ person.
   a) ❒ happy
   b) ❒ tidy
   c) ❒ satisfied

6. Jack's mouth opens in ______________.
   a) ❒ amazement
   b) ❒ anger
   c) ❒ disgust

Jack calls up the criminal files and tells the computer to search under the registration numbers for known criminals. The computer produces five names. Jack then does more checking and finds out that two of the five are in prison and one other is dead.

suspected	mutmaßlich; tatverdächtig

Roberta and Jack drive to the first address, but there is nobody home and the neighbour tells them that Mr and Mrs Hale are visiting their daughter in Australia. They won't be back for another four weeks.

Next, the detectives drive to the second address, which is in Chelsea. The owner of the car is Ali Ibrahim, a suspected criminal. Mrs Ibrahim answers the door and tells them that she hasn't seen Ali for a few days.

Roberta looks at the woman and can see that she is nervous.

"May we come in, Mrs Ibrahim?"

"Look. I tell you he's not here."

"We would like to come in anyway. We don't want the neighbours to hear everything."

Mrs Ibrahim looks at the next house and sees that the curtains are moving.

"Okay. If you must," she sighs.

Jack and Roberta enter the house.

Mrs Ibrahim turns to Roberta and Jack.

"Now that you're here, you might as well sit down. Would you like something to drink?"

Roberta sits down and smiles.

"Not for me, thank you."

Mrs Ibrahim looks at Jack and he shakes his head.

Roberta takes out a notepad and pencil.

"Now, Mrs Ibrahim," she begins, smiling. "When was the last time you saw your husband?"

Exercise 7: Unscramble the sentences. **Bringen Sie die Wörter in die richtige Reihenfolge!**

1. idea I an have

___

2. names computer five the produces

___

3. answers Ibrahim door the Mrs

___

4. enter and Roberta house the Jack

___

5. shop are at cars now police arriving the

___

"A few days ago," Mrs Ibrahim replies carefully.

"When exactly, Mrs Ibrahim?"

Suddenly there are screams from children upstairs. Mrs Ibrahim stands up, but Jack waves her back.

"I'll take care of them."

He goes up the stairs and Mrs Ibrahim doesn't look happy with the situation.

Roberta continues.

"What kind of car does your husband drive?"

"A white one."

"A white what?"

"Oh, I don't know. Something small."

"A Golf, maybe?" Roberta asks patiently.

"Yes. I think it's a Golf."

"And where does your husband work, Mrs Ibrahim?"

"He doesn't."

Roberta looks slowly around the living room.

"You have a lovely house. New stereo, new plasma television and very expensive furniture. Where does all this money come from, Mrs Ibrahim?"

"You ask Ali. I think his family has money."

That's all for now.	Das war's fürs Erste.

Exercise 8: Colour quiz. Übersetzen Sie die Farben und enträtseln Sie das Lösungswort!

1. rot ☐ _ _
2. gelb _ _ _ _ ☐ _
3. blau ☐ _ _ _
4. grün _ _ _ ☐ _
5. braun _ ☐ _ _ _
6. weiß _ _ _ ☐ _
7. schwarz _ _ ☐ _ _

Lösung: ☐☐☐☐☐☐☐

"That's nice. All right, that's all for now."

Mrs Ibrahim jumps up from the couch and runs to the foot of the stairs.

"Okay, children. You can come down now."

The children come **banging** down the stairs and Jack follows them. At the bottom, Fatima, the girl, grabs his hand and smiles at him lovingly.

to bang	knallen, poltern
dirty look	böser Blick
fortune	Vermögen
to trust	(ver)trauen
gut feeling	Bauchgefühl
headscarf	Kopftuch

Mrs Ibrahim picks up the girl and gives Jack a **dirty look**.

Roberta and Jack thank her and go back to their car. Jack starts the engine and says, "Jusuf, Mrs Ibrahim's son, is very lucky. His room is full of all the latest toys. They must have cost a **fortune**."

"Jack!"

"Where to, Roberta?"

"Switch the engine off, Jack."

"Why, Roberta? Did I do something wrong?"

"No Jack, you didn't. I think Mrs Ibrahim is lying to us. She seemed very nervous," Roberta replies.

> Achtung, Verwechslungsgefahr!
>
> Das englische Verb **to lie** bedeutet sowohl „lügen" als auch „liegen", allerdings werden die Formen von *to lie* (liegen) unregelmäßig gebildet *(lie, lay, lain)*.

"Well, I know she is lying. Jusuf told me that his dad was there at breakfast time, but maybe he was lying?"

"**Trust** me, Jack. My **gut feeling** tells me that Mrs Ibrahim knows where her husband is."

"Oh, Roberta. You know I don't believe in that sort of thing," Jack says.

"Look, Jack!"

Jack looks to where Roberta is pointing and sees Mrs Ibrahim, who is now wearing a **headscarf** and sunglasses, leave her house and hurry down the street.

Jack says in frustration, "Roberta, how do you do it?"

"It doesn't matter, Jack. She's walking towards the shops, but I don't think that she's going shopping. Look, she's wearing sunglasses."
"Should we follow her on foot?"
"No, Jack. She would recognize us. We'll follow her with the car but keep a few hundred yards back."
As Mrs Ibrahim turns the corner at the end of the street, Jack starts the car and drives slowly to the corner. They see Mrs Ibrahim cross the street and go into a pub next to a bakery. Jack knows the pub and he tells Roberta that a lot of criminal types meet there.
Jack parks the car outside the pub, and they look through the window. They see Mrs Ibrahim approach the bar and speak to a man. Roberta looks at one of the files that she brought with her and tells Jack that it's Ali Ibrahim.
Ali is talking angrily to his wife and she starts to cry, covering her face with her hands.

Exercise 9: Match up the opposites. **Welche Gegenteile gehören zusammen? Ordnen Sie zu!**

1. ☐ down	a) mum
2. ☐ top	b) expensive
3. ☐ wrong	c) laugh
4. ☐ dad	d) arrive
5. ☐ leave	e) bottom
6. ☐ cry	f) right
7. ☐ cheap	g) up

to tug	zupfen
assistance	Hilfe, Unterstützung
witness	Zeuge/Zeugin
entrance	Eingang
investigator	Ermittler

Jack **tugs** Roberta's sleeve. "Look, Roberta. There's a white Golf parked just down the street."

Roberta looks at the files in her hands. "That's the one we are looking for, Jack. It's registered to Ali Ibrahim. Let's call for some back-up."

Roberta calls for **assistance** and five minutes later, a green van arrives. A man in blue overalls gets out of the van and goes to the car.

"Excuse me, Madam. Are you Inspector Fletcher?"

"That's right. Are you our back-up?"

"Yes, Inspector. I'm Constable Simmons."

"Right, Constable. Are you alone?"

"No, Inspector. Woman Police Constable Kelly is in the van."

"Good. Come on, Jack."

They go to the van and Roberta tells Kelly to take their car back to the station. As she leaves, Mrs Ibrahim comes out of the pub and walks back towards her house. Jack and Roberta are in the back of the van, so they won't be recognized.

"Should I follow her, Inspector?"

"No, Constable. We're more interested in her husband."

Two minutes later, Ali Ibrahim leaves the pub, gets into the white Golf and drives off. Constable Simmons looks at Roberta.

"Would you like me to catch him, so that you can arrest him?"

"No, Constable. The **witness** at the newsagent's said that there were two foreign-looking men in the car. I'm hoping Mr Ibrahim will lead us to the other one."

The van follows him at a safe distance. Ten minutes later, Ali stops in front of a five-star hotel. He gets out of the car and starts talking to a man at the hotel **entrance**. Roberta is excited.

"Jack, I think that I know him."

"Are you sure, Roberta?"
"Yes. I've seen his face somewhere before. I just can't remember where."
Ali seems very nervous and suddenly turns round and points towards the van. The man talking to Ali looks at the van. Roberta catches her breath as his eyes meet hers. She feels like a rabbit in front of a snake.
Suddenly the man grabs Ali's arm and pulls him into the hotel.
Roberta and Jack jump out of the van and run to the hotel entrance. There is no sign of them in the lobby, and Jack asks the receptionist if he saw where the two men went. The receptionist points to the back of the hotel and tells Jack that the men left through the back door.
Roberta and Jack run to the door. It opens onto a side street behind the hotel. They look up and down the street, but the two men are gone. They walk back to the van and tell the driver to take them back to the station.

Exercise 10: Translation. Lesen Sie weiter und fügen Sie die Übersetzung der angegebenen Wörter ein!

When they get back to the **1. Büro** ________________, there is a message on Roberta's desk. It's from Mr Harris, the crime scene **investigator**. Roberta should ring him as soon as possible. She calls him **2. sofort** ________________.
"Hello, Mr Harris. It's Roberta Fletcher."
"Ah, Inspector Fletcher! We managed to get a fingerprint off the **3. Tür** ________________ handle at the newsagent's.

It could belong to anyone, but it's **4.** wahrscheinlich ______________ worth running it through your criminal records."

"Thanks, Mr Harris. When can you mail it to me?"

"It's already on its way to you."

Roberta's computer **5.** zeigt ______________ a received e-mail and she calls it up. The **6.** Fingerabdruck ______________________ is quite clear, and she runs it through the criminal records.

A few minutes **7.** später ______________________, "No matches" flashes on her screen.

Roberta rings the hotel where they lost Ali and asks them to fax her a guest list. She hangs up and looks over at Jack. He is busy looking through some files.

"Jack, the fingerprint isn't on the records. I think I will ring the hospital and see if they have finished the post-mortem examination yet."

"Good idea, Roberta. I need a coffee. Would you like one, too?"

"Yes please, Jack."

Jack leaves and Roberta calls the hospital.

"Hello. This is Inspector Fletcher. I'm in charge of the Giles murder case. Do you know if the post-mortem is finished?"

"I think it's still going on. I'll put you through to the autopsy room."

"Thanks very much."

"Autopsy room. John Bird speaking," a man's voice answers.
"Hello, Dr Bird. It's Roberta Fletcher here."
"Hello, Inspector."
"Did you finish the Giles post-mortem?"
"We're nearly finished."
"You see, I'm at a **dead end** and I was wondering if you could help? Any information would be **appreciated**."
"As you probably know, he was **strangled**. The interesting thing is that he seems to have been strangled with wire."
"That's interesting. Is it **common**?"
"Not at all. It was a common way to kill people twenty years ago, when most killers used piano wire, but this is my first since then. I'll send you a copy of the full report in about half an hour."
"That's great, Dr Bird. Thanks a lot."
Roberta puts the phone down as Jack comes back with the coffee. The fax machine starts to print as Jack gives her the coffee.

no matches	keine Treffer
to flash	(auf)blinken, blitzen
post-mortem (examination)	Obduktion
in charge (of)	zuständig (für); leiten
to put (sb.) through	(jmd.) durchstellen, verbinden (Telefon)
dead end	Sackgasse
to appreciate sth.	etw. zu schätzen wissen
strangled	erwürgt
common	häufig, (weit) verbreitet
hit	*hier*: Treffer

"Thanks, Jack. I hope that's the guest list from the hotel. Could you go through it, please? I want to run something through the Interpol file."
"Sure. No problem."
Roberta calls up the Interpol files. Under "method of killing", she types in "wire/piano wire". Ten seconds later she gets two **hits**.

The first is: "Jaques Bernod, assassin, born Marseilles, France, 1928, died Paris 1982."
The second is: "Marco, assassin, is suspected of at least five assassinations. Price per assassination believed to be 1 million dollars, preferred killing method: strangulation with piano wire, no further information available."

Exercise 11: Questions about the text. Beantworten Sie die Fragen zum Text!

1. Does Dr Bird work in the autopsy room?

   ____

2. Why does Roberta call the hospital?

   ____

3. Who owns a building company?

   ____

4. Why does Roberta clap her hands?

   ____

5. What does Jack get Roberta to drink?

   ____

6. What does Roberta call up on the Interpol files?

   ____

Roberta claps her hands. "Jack! It's Marco. There's a very unclear photo, but it's him. I recognize the eyes."
Jack walks over, grinning. "Roberta, I recognize this name on the guest list."
"Which one, Jack?" she asks.

"This one. Clive Hadley."
"Hadley. Isn't that the millionaire who owns a building company?"
"Yes. Don't you remember? We've been trying to get him for years. We are sure that he's an international arms dealer."
"Now I remember. We don't have any proof, do we?"

assassin	Auftragsmörder, Attentäter
assassination	Ermordung, Attentat
available	verfügbar
to clap	klatschen
proof	Beweis(e)
to scratch	kratzen

"No, but maybe we can get him this time!"
"I hope so, Jack. Now, you continue checking the guest list and I'll get Clive Hadley's file."
When Roberta comes back with Clive Hadley's file, Jack scratches his head. He tells her that he doesn't recognize any other names on the list.
"What's the connection to Hadley? Do you think Marco is in England to buy weapons off him?"
"I doubt it. He bought weapons from Giles."
"Jack. Look, I have an idea. Perhaps Marco is staying at Ibrahim's house?"
"It's worth checking. In any case, Mrs Ibrahim might know where to find him."
"Well, why don't you go over there and ask her?"
"Good idea, Roberta. I'll do it now."
Jack leaves and Roberta continues looking at the files. She is interrupted as the phone rings. It is Constable Simmons, her van driver. He tells her that he saw where Ali went. She tells him to wait for her at the entrance to the building. On the way down, she rings Jack and informs him.

3 The Chase

Exercise 12: Fill in the blanks. Lesen Sie weiter und setzen Sie die Wörter an der richtigen Stelle ein!

win | sister | photo | sure | man | upstairs | play

Jack arrives at the Ibrahims' and shows the **1.** ________ to Mrs Ibrahim.
"Sorry. I don't know this **2.** ________."
"Are you **3.** ________, Mrs Ibrahim?"
"Positive."
Just then, Jusuf and his **4.** ________, Fatima, come running down the stairs. Jusuf sees the photo in Jack's hand."
"Hello, Uncle Jack. What's that?"
"It's a game, Jusuf. Guess who it is and you **5.** ________ a sweet."
Mrs Ibrahim grabs Jusuf. "Get back **6.** ________, Jusuf, and take your sister with you."
"No, mummy. I want to **7.** ________ this game with Uncle Jack."

in defeat	niedergeschlagen
nameplate	Namensschild
to wipe	(ab)wischen
to bother sb.	jmd. belästigen
badge	Abzeichen

Jack puts his hand on Mrs Ibrahim's shoulder.
"Let them look, Mrs Ibrahim."
Mrs Ibrahim goes very pale and sits on the couch. Jack takes two sweets out of his pocket and turns to the children.
"Okay. Are you ready?" he asks, smiling.
They both nod and smile. Jack shows them the photo.
"It's Uncle Marco! We win. Give us the sweets!"
Jack gives them the sweets, sends them upstairs and turns to Mrs Ibrahim.
"Okay, Mrs Ibrahim. Now I want the truth, or I will have to arrest you and take your children to a children's home."
Mrs Ibrahim nods her head in defeat.
"I'll give you the address of the safe house, but I want you to promise me that Ali won't be hurt."
"I can't do that, Mrs Ibrahim. I can only tell you that the British Police don't hurt people, unless they absolutely have to."
Mrs Ibrahim looks into Jack's eyes, nods and tells him the address.

The address is only about two miles away and Jack quickly drives there. It's an old house set back from the road. Jack tries the door, but it's locked. There's a bell with no nameplate next to the door, so Jack pushes it. Jack hears the bell ring inside the house, but nobody answers it. He's just wondering what to do next when he hears a voice.
"Hey, you! What do you want?"
An old man comes from around the back of the house, wiping dirt from his hands.
"I'm sorry to bother you. I'm a police officer – here's my badge. I need to know who lives in this house."

spare key	Ersatzschlüssel
glove compartment	Handschuhfach
wardrobe	Kleiderschrank
envelope	Briefumschlag
signature	Unterschrift
signed	unterschrieben
to intend	beabsichtigen

"A man named Ali Ibrahim is renting it for two months."
"Right. Well, I need to search the house," Jack explains. "You do have a spare key, don't you?"
"Of course I do. I'll go and get it."
The old man goes to a car parked in front of the house and gets a bunch of keys from the glove compartment. He then lets Jack into the house. He turns to Jack.
"Mr Ibrahim's not in any trouble, is he?"
"Not yet. Listen, Mr...?"
"Devlin, Sam Devlin."
"Mr Devlin. Do you think I could have a few minutes alone to take a look around the flat?"
"Sure. No problem. I'll wait in the garden. Just shout when you're finished."
"Thanks a lot."
Jack walks into the living room, but it's empty except for a couch and a television. He goes past the kitchen and then through a door, which leads to a small bedroom.
There is a travel bag with a change of clothes on the bed. The wardrobe is empty. He pulls the drawer of the bedside table, but it sticks. He takes it out completely and sees an envelope taped to the bottom. He opens the envelope and sees a long list of weapons, including rockets. It's dated the fourth of June 1984 and the customer is a Colonel Jamirez. Jack is pretty sure that this will be the rebels' leader. He whistles and looks at the signature. It is signed by Clive Hadley. Suddenly his jacket pocket starts vibrating and he takes out his mobile phone.

Exercise 13: Compound nouns. **Bilden Sie zusammengesetzte Begriffe!**

1.	☐ living	a) table
2.	☐ safe	b) bell
3.	☐ police	c) phone
4.	☐ no	d) room
5.	☐ alarm	e) compartment
6.	☐ glove	f) officer
7.	☐ mobile	g) problem
8.	☐ bedside	h) house

"Hello?" Jack answers the call.

"Jack, it's me, Roberta. Are you at the Ibrahims'?"

"No, but I have proof that Clive Hadley is selling weapons. The document shows that he sold weapons to a Colonel Jamirez in 1984."

"Great! So Marco intends to kill Hadley?"

"That's almost certain. Where are you?"

"I'm following Ali's white Golf. Marco's in the car with him and it looks as though they are driving to Waterloo Bridge."

"Just a minute, Roberta. I read in the newspaper that Clive Hadley's building company is doing renovations on Waterloo Bridge."

"Yes, of course. This morning I read that the bridge is being reopened today."

"What time?"

"I'm quite sure they said 3 p.m."

armed	bewaffnet
at full speed	mit voller Geschwindigkeit
meanwhile	inzwischen, unterdessen
estate car	Kombiwagen
to skid	schleudern, rutschen
screech	Quietschen, Kreischen
groan	Stöhnen
forehead	Stirn
to need stitches	genäht werden müssen

"It's twenty-five past two now. I'll meet you there. I'm leaving as soon as my back-up gets here."

"Okay, Jack, but hurry! Neither of us is armed," Roberta says. "It would be too dangerous to try and arrest Marco and Ali at the moment."

Jack runs out of the house. He shouts thank you to Mr Devlin and gets in his car. He puts the blue light on the roof and drives off at full speed.

Meanwhile, Roberta and Constable Simmons are following Ali's car in a blue estate car. Roberta is sure that Ali knows they are behind him, because he is now driving faster.

"Can't you drive faster, Constable?"

"Sorry, Inspector. I can't. I'm driving as fast as I can."

Suddenly a lorry pulls out from a side street and Constable Simmons brakes very hard. The car skids with a screech of brakes and crashes into the lorry with a loud bang. Then there is silence.

Roberta shakes herself and starts to get out of the car, but the door is stuck. She hears a groan and looks across at Constable Simmons. His forehead is bleeding quite badly.

"Constable Simmons, are you okay?"

"I'm fine, Inspector. It's only a scratch."

"No, it isn't. You are bleeding quite heavily and I think you need stitches. I'll call for an ambulance immediately."

"No really, Inspector..."

"No arguing, Constable. You wait here for the ambulance. That's an order."

"Yes, Inspector," he replies weakly.
The traffic is standing still and drivers start **honking** their horns and shouting **abuse**.
As Roberta gets out of the car, a man with grey hair grabs her by the arm.
"Are you hurt? I'm a doctor. I can help."
"Doctor, could you **do me a favour**?"
"Yes, of course."
"Can you look after my driver until the ambulance gets here, please?"
"Of course."
"Thank you very much," she replies and turns around to go.
Roberta calls for an ambulance and then calls the station to arrange a road block on Waterloo Bridge. She looks around and sees a motorcyclist talking to the lorry driver. She runs across to them.
"Excuse me!"
The motorcyclist looks her up and down and **obviously** likes what he sees.
"Yes, my love?"
"First, I'm not your love, and second, I'm a police officer. Here's my **identity card**."
"Sorry, Officer. How can I help you?"
"I want you to take me to Waterloo Bridge as fast as you possibly can."
"What about **speed traps**?"
"If we get caught, I'll pay them."
"That's **fair enough**. Let's go," he laughs.

to honk	hupen
abuse	*hier*: Beschimpfung(en), Missbrauch
to do sb. a favour	jmd. einen Gefallen tun
obviously	offensichtlich
identity card	(Dienst-) Ausweis
speed trap	Radarfalle
fair enough	in Ordnung

Exercise 14: Choose the correct alternative. **Lesen Sie weiter und unterstreichen Sie jeweils die richtige Variante!**

Jack races away **1.** to / from the hotel and takes the **2.** slowest / fastest route to Waterloo Bridge. However, he's not in luck, because the rush hour traffic has **3.** begun / ended. He can't get past the cars, even though his blue light is flashing. He curses that he would probably be faster **4.** swimming / running. This gives him an idea. He thinks he could run to the **5.** pub / bridge in about ten minutes. He **6.** jumps / falls out of the car and starts **7.** running / walking. Behind him the car drivers are honking their horns, because Jack's car is now blocking them.

Jack **8.** cries / grins and whispers, "Sorry."

At the same time, Roberta is holding on to the motorcyclist for dear life. Horns are honking and drivers are shouting. She hears a woman scream and sees a mother holding her child as the motorcycle rushes past. Now she remembers why she didn't join the Motorcycle Police. She hates motorcycles!

to curse	fluchen
for dear life	um des nackten Lebens willen
to rush	eilen

4 Showdown on Waterloo Bridge

Ali and Marco are now only half a mile from Waterloo Bridge. Ali looks into the rearview mirror every few seconds.
Finally he says, "We lost them, Master."
"Good!"
Ali looks at Marco and sees that he looks very grim. Marco checks his gun again for the fifth time.
Ali looks up and sees that in front of them a couple of police cars are blocking the entrance to the bridge.
"Master, what should I do?"
"Drive!"
"But, Master?"
Marco leans over and presses Ali's right leg down. The car engine screams and the car shoots forward.
"Master, no!"
Marco then uses his other hand to grab the steering wheel and keep the car in a straight line.
Ali puts his hands to his face and starts praying.

rearview mirror	Rückspiegel
grim	grimmig, streng
steering wheel	Lenkrad
unconscious	bewusstlos

The car hits the back of a police car at full speed and there is a loud bang. The white Golf is badly damaged, but it is still going very fast. Ali is unconscious, but Marco presses his leg down again and steers for a Rolls Royce in the middle of the bridge. A man in a black suit, who is carrying a gun, jumps out of the Rolls Royce and shoots at the Golf. He jumps aside at the last second as the Golf crashes into the Rolls Royce at full force. There is the sound of screeching metal and steam is coming out from under the Golf's bonnet.

to take aim	zielen
to stumble	stolpern
to wipe out	auslöschen
unbearable	unerträglich

Marco dives out of the car holding his gun. He rolls on the ground as the bodyguard moves from behind the Golf. The bodyguard shoots, but Marco is already rolling. He stops, takes careful aim and shoots the bodyguard. Marco starts to walk to the Rolls Royce and realizes that his right leg doesn't work. He looks down in surprise and sees his trousers are covered in blood. Then the pain comes. But he stumbles on towards the Rolls Royce.

Clive Hadley is sitting in the back and is shaking with fear.

"Who are you? Please don't kill me."

"My name is Marco. You sold rockets to Colonel Jamirez twenty years ago. One of those rockets killed my family. You have their blood on your hands and you'll die for it."

"Please. You don't have to kill me."

"Give me one reason why I shouldn't, Hadley."

"It was only a business deal."

"It was a business deal that wiped out my family and thousands of others."

"I just wanted to make a bit of money."

"A bit of money! You made millions by causing thousands of deaths!" Marco shouts.

Hadley starts begging. "Marco, please. How much do you want? I'll pay anything you ask. One million, two million? Name your price and the money is yours!"

Marco's pain is now almost unbearable, but he smiles.

"You can't buy me, Hadley. You **caused** so much pain and death over the years. Well, now it's your turn."
Marco sees the fear disappear from Hadley's face and, at the same time, hears a noise behind him. He turns around.

Exercise 15: Definitions. Enträtseln Sie die folgenden Definitionen!

1. The motor of a car. ____________________
2. Someone who protects people. ____________________
3. The number one plus six zeros. ____________________
4. It has two wheels and an engine. ____________________
5. If you are suddenly gone, you ... ____________________

Roberta and Jack arrive at the entrance to the bridge at the same time. Jack is breathing heavily and Roberta is feeling very **dizzy** from the motorcycle ride.
They both turn to look at the scene on the bridge. There seem to **be smashed** and smoking cars everywhere.
Roberta can see Marco leaning into the Rolls Royce talking to somebody. Out of the corner of her eye she sees movement. There is a man in a dark suit who is **creeping** very slowly from behind the Rolls Royce. He has a gun in his hand and is walking towards Marco!
She knows she shouldn't, but she really wants to shout a warning to Marco. Before she can react, there is a loud scream.
"Hey!"

to cause	verursachen
dizzy	schwindlig
smashed	zertrümmert
to creep	schleichen, kriechen

to distract	ablenken
strength	Kraft, Stärke
sweat	Schweiß
mercy	Erbarmen, Gnade
to kneel down	sich hinkien
to presume	vermuten, annehmen

It's Ali. He is standing in front of the Golf and shouting to distract the bodyguard.

There is the sound of two gunshots, and Marco and the bodyguard fall to the ground. The bodyguard doesn't move, but Marco crawls back towards the Rolls Royce.

Clive Hadley panics and tries to get out of the car on the side away from Marco, but the door has been blocked by the crash.

Roberta, Jack and Ali start running towards Marco shouting for him to stop. Marco ignores them and with the last of his strength, pulls himself to the door of the car.

Clive Hadley is still trying to open the car door. His face is covered in sweat and he's calling for his mother. Suddenly he sees Marco's head appear at the other door and he screams.

"Marco, no! Please have mercy!"

Marco shakes his head. "No mercy, Hadley. Revenge is mine!"

He shoots Hadley in the head and falls back onto the floor.

Roberta kneels down next to Marco's body, when suddenly Marco coughs and opens his eyes. He smiles through his pain.

"The police, I presume?"

"That's right, Marco."

"I was right to kill Hadley. There is proof in my room at the safe house."

"We got it, Marco. Don't talk, the ambulance is coming."

Marco tries to laugh, but it turns into a bloody cough. "Too late. I can already hear her voice."

"Whose?"

"My sister's. Jasmin..."

Roberta feels Marco's body relax and wipes a tear from her eye.

A Nice Neighbourhood

Sarah Trenker

1 A Meeting in the Church

It is cold in the church hall and their breath comes out in little clouds. Detective Frank Durham pulls up the collar of his leather jacket and glances at his partner. Barry smiles and just shrugs his shoulders.

None of the six men around the table speak. They just wait. Police Constable Jones, Dr Sterling, Mr Monks and Mr Philips sit on one side of the table, the two detectives on the other. The only person missing is the mayor.

Barry wishes he had a bigger chair. He is a heavy man and his wooden chair creaks loudly as he tries to find a more comfortable position.

church hall	Gemeindehalle
to glance at	(an)schauen
to shrug (one's shoulders)	die Achseln zucken
constable	Polizist, Wachtmeister
mayor	Bürgermeister
to creak	knarren; quietschen
impatiently	ungeduldig

"How much longer do you think the mayor is going to be?" asks Frank impatiently. "Wouldn't it be better to call him?"

"I already have," replies Mr Monks. "He said he was in the middle of another meeting and would come as quickly as he could."

"We could start without him," suggests Mr Philips.

"No, no, Mr Ainsley wouldn't like that," the constable replies.

At last the door opens and the mayor walks in. With his long, dark-

blue coat over his suit, and an umbrella in his hand, he looks more like a London **stockbroker** than a village mayor.
Frank dislikes him immediately.
"Sorry I am late," says the mayor in a voice that does not sound sorry at all.
He walks over to the table. "You must be Detectives Durham and Andrews, I **presume**," he says and smiles at his little joke.

Exercise 1: Adjectives. Steigern Sie die folgenden Adjektive. Beachten Sie die Beispiele im Text!

1. big ______________ ______________
2. comfortable ______________ ______________
3. heavy ______________ ______________
4. cold ______________ ______________
5. good ______________ ______________
6. slow ______________ ______________

"And you are Mark Ainsley, the VILLAGE mayor, I presume," answers Frank dryly.
"Just so, just so," says the mayor. The smile dies on his lips as he reads Frank's **expression**. "As I said, sorry you had to wait. Let's **get straight down to business**."
He sits down and Barry opens his notebook on a clean page.

stockbroker	Aktienhändler, Börsenmakler
to presume	vermuten, annehmen
expression	(Gesichts-) Ausdruck
to get (straight) down to business	(gleich) zur Sache kommen

Frank is about to speak when the mayor interrupts him. "Perhaps you should just ask us the questions and we can tell you all we know, can't we?" He looks round at the other men who all nod. Frank takes another breath.

to nod	nicken
to sign	unterzeichnen
death certificate	Sterbeurkunde
cause of death	Todesursache
coincidence	Zufall
to report	melden, berichten; anzeigen
suspicion	Verdacht
post-mortem (examination)	Obduktion

"On the other hand," continues the mayor and places his hands in front of him, "perhaps it is easier if we just tell you what we know. What would you prefer?"

"I think, mayor, if you don't mind, I'll ask the questions," Frank says quickly before the mayor can come up with a third choice.

"Now, my information so far is that three men have died here in Little Meadow in the course of the last two months. The last man, Michael Reed, died on Monday. Is that right?"

"Yes, Monday evening," replies PC Jones.

"And after this third death you began to wonder about the causes of the deaths of Nicholas Fields and Tony Edmonton, is that right?"

"Yes."

"Dr Sterling, you signed the death certificates of all three men, I believe. What made you change your opinion about the cause of death?"

"I knew all three men," answers the doctor. "They were all patients of mine at one time or another. They had stress at work like a lot of men of their age but otherwise were in the best of health. So when the third one died, it seemed too much of a coincidence."

"And that is why you reported your suspicions to the mayor?"

"Yes."

"Did you do a post-mortem examination on any of the men?"

"No. I am a general practitioner; I can't really do a proper post-mortem. However, I did notice that all of the corpses had yellow tongues. At first, I just thought it was because of rigor mortis, but now I am not so sure."

Frank looks at Barry. "You saw enough bodies when you worked with that team in London. Is a yellow tongue a typical sign of rigor mortis?"

"Not really," answers Barry. "I think we should let one of the doctors in town look at the bodies."

"BODY," corrects the mayor. "We cremated Nicholas Fields and Tony Edmonton."

"Oh great!" mutters Frank.

"Well, they weren't church-goers, you see," explains the mayor.

"And there is so little space in the graveyard. Anyway – the men were all new in the village."

"New?" Barry is surprised. "When I spoke to PC Jones on the phone yesterday, he told me that they all moved to Little Meadow about two years ago."

"Yes, well, that still makes them new to this village," answers the mayor.

"Most of the families who live here have been here for generations. We have a very close-knit community."

"So close that you don't like NEW people moving into the village?" asks Frank.

"No, no, that's not what I meant." The mayor looks a little embarrassed.

general practitioner	Allgemeinmediziner, Hausarzt
proper	ordentlich; passend
rigor mortis	Leichenstarre
body	*hier*: Leiche
to cremate	einäschern
to mutter	(vor sich hin)murmeln, brummeln
churchgoer	Kirchgänger
graveyard	Friedhof
close-knit community	enge Gemeinschaft
embarrassed	verlegen

Exercise 2: Translation. **Lesen Sie weiter und unterstreichen Sie die englische Übersetzung der angegebenen Wörter!**

Größe Metzger stirbt Plakate außerhalb

Frank **changes the subject**. "Where is Michael Reed now?"
Mr Philips, a red-faced man who manages to make even Barry look **slim**, holds up a hand the size of a small football. "He's in my fridge. I'm the village butcher. When somebody dies, we always put them in my fridge. That way we don't have to drive them to the next town and then back again."
"Yes, that is more practical."
Frank suddenly feels like he is in some **kind** of historical novel. It is all too **weird**. There is a butcher who is also the **undertaker**, a friendly policeman who says he doesn't own a gun, and a mayor who acts like a king. The village is so small that there isn't even a post office. And the posters outside the church show that the Christmas play is a big **annual** event...

to change the subject	das Thema wechseln
slim	schlank
kind	Art Sorte
weird	seltsam; unheimlich
undertaker	Bestatter
annual	jährlich
case	*hier*: Fall

He looks over at Mr Monks.
"Mr Monks, what do you know about this **case**?"
A man of only about 25, Mr Monks has a face that already shows the first **wrinkles** of frustration – and it is easy to see that he is not happy with life.

When he speaks it is like listening to a slow **whine**.
"I knew the three men well. I **used to** work for a bank in Gorleston-on-Sea. The three were all investment experts and..."
"Investment experts?" interrupts Frank. "What do you mean by 'investment experts'? Did they work at the bank, too?"
"No, they didn't," answers Mr Monks **irritably**. "They drove round all the villages here. They gave people investment tips."
"Investment tips?"
Mr Monks **sighs** as if it is so hard to deal with such idiots. "Yes. You know, someone comes to your home and tells you how to invest your **savings** to get the most out of the money."

wrinkle	Falte, Fältchen
whine	Gejammer
used to do sth.	etw. (früher) getan haben
irritably	gereizt
to sigh	seufzen
savings *pl*	Ersparnisse
to sense	spüren, fühlen
to bother sb.	jmd. belästigen
to murder	(er)morden
suspicious	misstrauisch; verdächtig
to wash one's dirty linen in public	seine schmutzige Wäsche in der Öffentlichkeit waschen

Mr Monks pauses. "Or at least that is what good investment experts do."
"Which these three weren't?" Frank **senses** that he is about to learn a possible motive.
Before Mr Monks can continue, however, the mayor interrupts him. "Now, now, Mr Monks. There's no need to **bother** the detectives with all of that unless we know that someone really did **murder** them." He turns to Frank. "Detective Durham, the fact that the three men were not particularly popular in the village was also something that made Dr Sterling and me **suspicious**. But perhaps it would be better to discuss that after your people have examined Mr Reed's body. Otherwise there is really no need for us to **wash our dirty linen in public**."

to frown	die Stirn runzeln
amusement	Vergnügung, Unterhaltung

The mayor gives Mr Monks a warning look and the younger man frowns silently.

Not all perfect in this village then after all, thinks Frank with slight amusement. He stands up. "Well, gentlemen, thank you for your time. I shall send a car over to collect Mr Reed from Mr Philips first thing tomorrow morning. We should have the results of the post-mortem by the afternoon."

Exercise 3: Used to. Formulieren Sie Fragen mit used to zu folgenden Sätzen!

1. Mr Monks now works for a company in Norwich.

   Where did he use to work?

2. I can now drive to work because I have a car.

   How ______________________________

3. The detectives can now contact each other with their mobile phones.

   How ______________________________

4. The village didn't have a post office until 1991.

   Where ______________________________

5. During the summer Mr Philips received his patients in the village hall.

   When ______________________________

to wave (one's hands)	winken; schwenken
safety belt	Sicherheitsgurt
to chuckle	kichern, glucksen
ingredient	Zutat; Bestandteil
winding	(sich) biegend, windend
nothing... but	nichts als, nur
puzzled	verblüfft, verwirrt

"Will you phone us, Detective?" asks the mayor.
"Yes."
PC Jones walks out to the car with them. "It seems so hard to believe that there could be a murderer living here," he says. He waves his hand at the quiet village streets and the fields in the background.
"There hasn't been a murder here since 1924. This is a very peaceful place, you know?"
In the car, Barry pulls the safety belt over his stomach and sits back gratefully into the comfortable seat.
"Strange people, aren't they?" he chuckles.
Frank grins and rubs his hands together to try and get them warm.
"They certainly are."
"Do you think it was murder?" replies Barry.
Frank starts the car. "Oh, I think so. Three healthy but unpopular men suddenly die in a village that doesn't like strangers. That certainly sounds like the perfect ingredients for murder to me."
They take the long winding road back through the fields and small villages towards the town. For half an hour, they see nothing on the road but a tractor and three girls on ponies.
Barry is puzzled. "Why would three investment experts come and live out in the middle of the East Anglian countryside, I wonder?"

Achten Sie auf den Unterschied zwischen **countryside** und **landscape:**
countryside bedeutet „Land, ländliche Gegend". Mit **landscape** bezeichnet man dagegen jede Art von Landschaft, z.B.
urban landscape Stadtlandschaft

"Easy pickings probably," answers Frank, as he lights yet another cigarette. "A lot of hard-working people with money they don't know what to do with!"

easy pickings *pl*	leichte Beute

Exercise 4: True or false? Welche Aussagen sind korrekt? Kreuzen Sie an!

1. The name of the village the detectives visit is Little Meadow. ❐
2. It is quite hot in the church hall. ❐
3. Detective Durham likes the mayor. ❐
4. Mr Monks worked for a bank in Great Yarmouth. ❐
5. The village undertaker is also the village butcher. ❐

2 Dirty Linen

Frank's office is chaotic. There are papers everywhere, photos of criminals on the wall and a bin full of empty cigarette packets and pizza boxes. He and Barry are reading a report about a theft in a restaurant in Great Yarmouth when someone knocks on the door.

"Come in," shouts Frank.

Ann Forest walks in. She is the pathologist, and she and Frank get on very well.

"Hi, you two, I've got the results for you."

theft	Diebstahl
pathologist	Gerichtsmedizinerin
to get on (with sb.)	(mit jmd.) auskommen
pigsty	Schweinestall
poison	Gift
serious	ernst

"And?" says Barry. He puts down the report he has in his hand and stands up to offer Ann his chair. She looks around and shakes her head.

"I'm not sitting down in this pigsty. Goodness knows what sort of bacteria are hiding in this room," she says and grins.

"Have it your own way," answers Frank, who also grins. "So, was it murder?"

"Oh yes, it was certainly murder. Poison."

"And what sort of poison was it?" Frank asks, suddenly serious.

"Rat poison," answers the young pathologist.

"You mean like warfarin?" asks Barry.

victim	Opfer
to swallow	schlucken
obviously	offensichtlich
dose	Dosis
to dissolve	(sich) auflösen, verflüssigen
Egyptian mummy	ägyptische Mumie
to dehydrate	austrocknen, Wasser entziehen
St Peter's gates	Himmelspforte

"Yes," answers Ann. "Although not many people use warfarin today because there are a lot of better alternatives on the market. But there was some warfarin in the victim's body."

"Wouldn't a person know if they swallowed rat poison?"

"Oh no! Mixed in a cup of tea, for example, the victim would not notice a thing – well, until later. Funnily enough, doctors now use warfarin for people with heart problems – obviously in small doses."

"And Mr Reed's dose?" Frank types W-A-R-F-A-R-I-N into the search engine as he asks Ann the question.

Ann has a look at her notes. "Absolutely deadly... Mr Reed swallowed enough to kill at least five men. Anyway, you can read all you need to know about warfarin in my notes here. It is a very effective poison. It dissolves in water and, as I said, anyone who takes it will not taste it."

Barry looks down into his mug of tea. "You mean I could be drinking it now and would not know about it?"

"That's right," replies Ann and grins again.

Frank stands up and takes the notes from the pathologist. "Anything else you can tell us?"

"Yes. The body looks a bit like an Egyptian mummy. That is very typical of rat poison. It dehydrates the victim. Normally, if a victim gets to a hospital quickly enough, it is possible to save him. But Mr Reed's stomach also contained a lot of sleeping powder. He probably didn't know anything about the poison until he found himself in front of St Peter's gates."

"Assuming, of course, that he went to heaven," replies Frank dryly.
"Exactly!"

Exercise 5: Odd one out. **Welches Wort ist das „schwarze Schaf"?**

1. tidy | clean | chaotic | washed
2. full | nothing | empty | unfilled
3. heart | brain | football | stomach
4. pigsty | pond | house | zoo
5. cocktail | juice | tea | meal
6. thief | constable | policeman | detective

After Ann leaves the office, Frank reaches for the phone. He dials the number the mayor gave him. A secretary answers the phone.

"This is Detective Durham. I would like to speak to Mark Ainsley, please."

"Ah yes, Detective. The mayor is expecting your call. I shall put you through."

"Good afternoon, Detective Durham. Mark Ainsley speaking. Have you got the results for us?"

"Yes. You were right to be suspicious. It was murder."

"Oh damn!" exclaims the mayor. "So what do we do now?"

to assume	vermuten, annehmen
to dial	wählen (Telefon)
to put (sb.) through	(jmd.) durchstellen, verbinden (Telefon)
↯ damn	↯ verdammt, verflucht
to exclaim	(aus)rufen

"Detective Andrews and I will come back to the village tomorrow and start the investigation. It would be very helpful if you could get your secretary to make a photocopy of all the information you have about the three men, their addresses, date of arrival in the village, job, and so on."

investigation	Ermittlung, Untersuchung
horse breeder	Pferdezüchter
villager	Dorfbewohner(in)
to remind sb. (of sth.)	jmd. (an etw.) erinnern
to be on one's own	auf sich allein gestellt sein
recently	kürzlich, jüngst

"Yes, yes, of course," answers the mayor. "There is a room here that you can use, if you wish. We don't really have a proper police station or village hall here. I have an office on the ground floor of my house. There are two rooms. Police Constable Jones uses one of the rooms for his papers but, as you know, we all have a number of different jobs. I earn my money as a horse breeder..."

"Yes, I know," answers Frank impatiently, who does not wish to hear another list of all the jobs the villagers do.

"I'm only reminding you," answers the mayor in a snobbish voice, "because I have to drive to Norwich tomorrow morning to sell a couple of horses. Miss Robins, my secretary, will let you in and show you the office, but you will be on your own until the afternoon."

"That will not be a problem, Mr Ainsley," says Frank, happy that he is going to have a chance to look through the information about the three men without the mayor around.

"I'll see you tomorrow afternoon then."

Frank puts the phone down and looks at Barry. "Can you look on the Internet and see if you can find out anything about the three investment experts – or any investment scandals recently? It is time to examine the dirty linen!"

Barry nods. "Right you are. I'll get down to it straight away."

Exercise 6: Choose the correct alternative. Lesen Sie weiter und unterstreichen Sie die richtige Variante!

Punctually at 9 a.m. the following morning, Frank and Barry walk up the concrete steps of the mayor's house and **1.** ring / dial the doorbell. A young secretary with red hair and a big smile opens the door.
"Are you the two detectives here to find out which of us is a **2.** churchgoer / murderer ?" she shouts.
"That's right, Miss Robins. That's us," Franks says, smiling at this welcome.
"Come in, please. I'll **3.** show / tell you the office."
She leads them to a small office at the back of the house. It is not big, but it is very **4.** light / dark and has a nice view of the garden.
"I have put everything I could find about the men on the table," Miss Robins remarks and points to some **5.** clothes / papers .
"There's also a list of **6.** anyone / everyone in the village and their telephone numbers. Mr Ainsley says you are welcome to use the phone."

"Perfect. That is very kind of him," Barry says.
"Would you like a coffee?"
"Yes, please. That would be great."
While Miss Robins goes to get the coffee, Frank and Barry look through the papers on the table.

according to	laut, zufolge
headline	Schlagzeile
suspicion	Verdacht
malpractice	Berufsvergehen; Amtsmissbrauch
magistrate	Amtsrichter
insurance	Versicherung
payment	(Be-)Zahlung
commission	*hier*: Provision; Kommission
contract	Vertrag
disgusting	ekelhaft
tray	Tablett

"**According to** these documents, they all arrived in the village at the same time," says Barry.

"And they were partners," adds Frank. "They set up their partnership twelve years ago in Lowestoft and then moved here two years ago."

"Hey, look at this!" Barry holds up a photocopy of a page in a newspaper. "This shows that the rich farmers were not the only reason the three partners moved out here."

Frank takes the cutting from Barry and quickly looks through it. There is a big **headline**: **Suspicion** of **malpractice**. Underneath it there is a long text about three men who had appeared before the **magistrate** in Lowestoft.

"This says the men got lots of old people to invest in life **insurance** that was only any good for young people. That means the only people helped by the insurance **payments** were the insurance company and the investment experts. Apparently some insurance companies pay particularly high **commission** for such **contracts**."

"**Disgusting**," mutters Barry and frowns.

At that moment Miss Robins comes into the room with the coffee. She sees the photocopy in Frank's hands.

"Yes, a nice trio, weren't they?"

"Did people here know about this when the three moved here?" asks Frank.

Miss Robins puts the **tray** of coffee on the table and frowns. "No, of course not. That's why they all moved out here. These men knew country people are very trusting and that they could just carry on where they had left off."

Miss Robins snorts angrily.

"My grandma lost a lot of money. She has real difficulties paying for her shopping now."

"So there was quite a bit of bad feeling towards the men?" Frank observes.

"Bad feeling! Hatred would be a better word." Miss Robins bangs the milk jug on the table next to the two mugs of coffee and the sugar.

"Didn't people try to do anything about it?" asks Barry.

"Yes and no," answers Miss Robins. "It was a long time before people realized what had happened. Then it was too late. Anyway, there was nothing that anyone could do. They didn't do anything illegal. It is not as if they held a gun to people's heads. We are simple country people, Detectives. We tend to believe what people say to us."

Barry nods sympathetically.

"So a lot of people lost money to them."

"Yes. All of the pensioners in the village, well, except Mrs Hutchinson. And a lot of younger people, too."

"Well, surely life insurance isn't bad for younger people," suggests Barry.

Miss Robins sighs. "Yes, that is why the three did not sell life insurance to them. They got them interested in some sort of property investment that went very wrong."

"Property investment?" Frank asks.

trusting	vertrauensvoll
to snort	schnauben, prusten
bad feeling	*hier*: böses Blut
to observe	feststellen, beobachten
hatred	Hass
to bang	knallen
property	*hier*: Immobilien; Eigentum; Eigenschaft

capable of	fähig, in der Lage zu
to sip	nippen, trinken
smart	*hier*: schick
elderly	ältere(r), ältlich
brightly	*hier*: freudig, fröhlich; hell

Miss Robins shrugs. "I don't know much about it. You'll have to ask the mayor, or you could ask my neighbour Fiona Chambers. She used to work for Paul & Son Architects. She was in love with Nicholas Fields, but he didn't love her. He just used her to get the information he wanted. She even invested some of her money in his projects. And then, of course, there was Mr Monks. You met him yesterday, I believe?"

"Yes, that's right," Frank replies.

"Mr Monks lost his job at the bank in Gorleston-on-Sea because of the three of them. He really hated them – not that I think he is capable of murder," Miss Robins adds quickly.

Frank nods. "I still think it would be good to speak to him and Miss Chambers. When is a good time to see them?"

Miss Robins shrugs her shoulders again. "Anytime really. They're both still looking for new jobs, so they are at home a lot of the time."

Frank looks at Barry, who is sipping his coffee. "A good place to start, perhaps? We can go and talk to Miss Chambers and Mr Monks now and be back in time to talk to the mayor when he gets back from Lowestoft."

"Hardly a lot going on here, is there?" remarks Frank, as he and Barry walk down the main street to where the mayor's secretary said they would find Miss Chambers.

There is one car parked outside the small shop next to the butcher's. Inside the shop, Frank and Barry can see a smart elderly lady talking to the young shop assistant.

"I don't think that shop assistant would survive for very long in a busy supermarket in Norwich," chuckles Barry in reply.

Exercise 7: Synonyms. **Finden Sie die Synonyme und setzen Sie die richtige Ziffer ein!**

1. hate	☐	cup
2. murder	☐	remark
3. mug	☐	three people
4. happen	☐	dislike
5. say	☐	take place
6. trio	☐	kill

As they pass the shop, the elderly lady customer comes trotting out towards them. She walks with a stick but holds her back very straight. She smiles brightly at the detectives.

"Good morning, young men, my name is Mrs Hutchinson. I hear you are here to find our murderer. How exciting! Of course, I know a lot about the three gentlemen, so do let me know if you need to ask me any questions. I am sure I can help you."

Frank is amused. News obviously travels very fast here. (i) He looks at Mrs Hutchinson and smiles. "We have only just started the investigation. But, yes, thank you for your offer. Where do you live, Mrs Hutchinson?"

"Just over there in the blue house," she answers, and points to the house with her stick.

> Im Englischen gibt es einige Substantive, die abweichend vom Deutschen nur im Singular gebraucht werden. Dazu gehören u. a. **news, information** und **knowledge.**
>
> *Bad news travels fast.* - Schlechte Nachrichten verbreiten sich schnell.
>
> *This information was not satisfactory.* - Diese Informationen waren nicht zufriedenstellend.
>
> *His knowledge of English is excellent.* - Seine Englischkenntnisse sind hervorragend.

"Would four o'clock be a good time for us to come round?" asks Frank politely.

"If you come around four, you can have tea with me. But please don't keep me waiting, young man. I like to eat at the same time every day. My digestion isn't what it was."

digestion	Verdauung

Frank nods and tries not to laugh. "If we are going to be late, I will let you know, Mrs Hutchinson," he says and watches the old lady walk slowly across the road to the blue house on the other side.

3 You Can't Choose Your Neighbours

The little brown cat playing on the sofa is more enthusiastic about the presence of the two detectives than Miss Chambers is. A middle-aged woman with a big nose and no taste in lipstick, Miss Chambers offers them tea but does not seem to want to speak.

In the lounge, Frank remains standing. "Thank you for seeing us at such short notice, Miss Chambers," he says.

"It is my duty," answers Miss Chambers and frowns unhappily.

"Quite right," mutters Frank. "Can you tell us how you knew the three victims?"

Miss Chambers sniffs. "I'm sure you already know that I was in love with Nicholas Fields. He asked me to marry him."

The woman brushes some imaginary crumbs off the table before she continues. "We met when I worked for Paul & Son Architects. Nicholas seemed such a wonderful man."

Detective Durham lifts an eyebrow to pretend interest.

"Were you still engaged at the time of his death, Miss Chambers?"

presence	Anwesenheit, Gegenwart
middle-aged	mittleren Alters
lounge	Wohnzimmer; Gesellschaftsraum
at such short notice	so kurzfristig
to sniff	schniefen
imaginary	imaginär, eingebildet
crumb	Brösel
to pretend	vorgeben, vortäuschen
engaged	verlobt; besetzt

"No," she replies. "When I decided to change jobs so I could have more time for him, Nicholas suddenly changed. I thought he would be happy to hear that I had a new job that meant I could be home by 6 p.m. – but he wasn't. He said it was boring because I no longer had anything exciting to talk about." Miss Chambers sniffs again.
"What did he find so exciting about hearing you talk about your job with the architects?" Frank asks gently.

gently	sanft, zärtlich
old maid	alte Jungfer
Serves them right!	Das geschieht ihnen recht!
to comment	(etw.) kommentieren
tap	Wasserhahn

"He wanted to know what sort of projects we had and whether there was any new business coming to the area. I thought it was because he wanted to find out how much I understood about his business – but I was wrong. I realized later that it was simply because he wanted to use the information I gave him for some new investment scheme he and his friends had thought up. He laughed at me when I told him I was in love with him and that I thought he wanted to marry me. He said I was a silly old maid who didn't know the difference between an innocent flirt and true love. He packed up all of my things from his house and left them on my doorstep, would you believe?"
Miss Chambers sniffs again. "But although I hated him and his partners, I didn't kill them," she adds. "Anyway, how did they die?"
"Poison," answers Frank.
"Serves them right!" comments Miss Chambers, with a satisfied expression on her face.
Embarrassed, Barry coughs. "I need a glass of water," he says and stands up. "May I get one in the kitchen?"
Miss Chambers nods and Barry walks through into the kitchen. For a moment the only sound is of running water as Barry turns the tap on in the kitchen.

Frank tries to change the subject a bit.
"Do you know if either Michael Reed or Tony Edmonton had girlfriends?" he asks.
"None of them had steady girlfriends. Nicholas laughed and said that perhaps I would make an honest man of him after all. He and his friends laughed a lot when he said that. Now I know the joke was on me."
Barry walks back in and sits down. He looks slightly pale. "I see you have a big bag of rat poison in the kitchen. Do you have problems with rats here?"
Miss Chambers is surprised and quite obviously annoyed at a question which shows Barry has been looking around her kitchen. "Yes, we all do. That is the disadvantage of living out in the middle of the countryside between fields on one side and a stream on the other. The rat population is enormous here. Last year I had a family of them in my big flowerpot in the garden. At night they used to come out and play with one another. It was impossible to sleep. That was why I bought the warfarin. It's good stuff – and has certainly solved a few rat problems for me!"
There is something menacing and creepy about the way Miss Chambers says "rat problems" and Frank feels a cold shiver go down his spine. He looks at Barry and nods to show that he is ready to go.

↯ the joke is on me	↯ ich bin die/der Dumme
pale	blass, bleich
annoyed	verärgert
disadvantage	Nachteil
stream	Bach
enormous	riesig, enorm
to solve	lösen; aufklären
menacing	bedrohlich
shiver	Schauer; Zittern
spine	Rückgrat

Outside, Barry chuckles.
"She reminds me of that story of Nancy Astor and Winston Churchill," he says as they walk back down towards the high street.

Exercise 8: Translation. Lesen Sie weiter und übersetzen Sie die angegebenen Wörter!

"Nancy Astor?"

"Yes. She was the first **female** member in the **House of Commmons**. She and Winston Churchill loved to argue. She **1.** einmal ________________ said to him, 'If I were your wife, I would put poison in your coffee', to which Winston Churchill replied, 'If I were your **2.** Ehemann ________________, I would drink it!'"

Laughing, the two detectives walk on to Mr Monks's home in Shepherd Street. Thankfully, Mr Monks does not offer them coffee, tea or **3.** Kekse ________________. Instead he asks them to sit at his table in the **4.** Küche ________________. There are lots of job **applications** lying on the **5.** Tisch ________________.

"Perhaps you can tell us how you lost your job at the bank?" Frank asks.

"**Stupidity**, really," answers Mr Monks, the lines of frustration deepening in his face. "It can get a bit **6.** einsam ________________ out here when you are single. Tony Edmonton started to invite me round for drinks with his two **7.** Freunde ________________."

"You know, they talked about their work and were also very interested in my work. It was nice to have someone to talk to..." Mr Monks hesitates.

He wipes his brow and then continues. "To start with, I didn't realize they just wanted information from me so they could do a bit of insider trading. By the time I did realize, it was too late. When I went to tell my boss about the three of them, he just thought I wanted to save my own skin. He fired me anyway. I shall never be able to work in a bank again."

"What did Mr Edmonton and the others say when you told them you no longer had a job?" Frank questions.

Mr Monks frowns. "They were sympathetic. They even took me out for a meal, but that was it. From one day to the next the phone calls stopped. When I phoned, they didn't have time for me."

"And how often did you see them after the meal?" Frank watches a nervous twitch on the young man's cheek.

"In a small village like this, you see everyone regularly – whether you want to or not," mutters Mr Monks. "I often saw the three of them driving through the village or in the shop. They would say hello, but that was it."

Mr Monks starts to write angrily in the corner of one of the applications.

Suddenly he looks up and stares directly at Frank. "Those three caused a lot of trouble here in the village. We should have listened to Mrs Hutchinson. She said they meant trouble – and she was right!"

female	weiblich
House of Commons	britisches Unterhaus
application	Bewerbung
stupidity	Dummheit
to wipe	(ab)wischen
insider trading	Insiderhandel (mit Aktien)
to save one's own skin	seine eigene Haut retten
↯ to fire sb.	↯ jmd. feuern
twitch	Zucken, Zuckung
to stare	starren
to cause	verursachen

"Hmm. Just one more question, Mr Monks. We hear that most people in Little Meadow have problems with rats. Is that true?"
"Er yes, yes that's right," Mr Monks answers. "The last couple of winters have been very warm. Rats are also very intelligent. If one rat eats some poison and dies, the others will not touch the poison. It's only very silly rats that eat warfarin in this area. We've all been trying out some new stuff recently."
"Oh, have you, now?" Frank asks. "And can you tell me what that is? Barry, please write it down."
Barry gets out his notebook.
"Brodifacoum – B-R-O-D-I-F-A-C-O-U-M. It is good because the rats just dehydrate very slowly, so even if they do die somewhere in the house, there is no smell."

Exercise 9: Fill in the blanks. **Vervollständigen Sie die folgenden Sätze!**

mayor | wearing | poison | lives | twitch | papers

1. Detective Durham learns that it is rat ______ that killed the three investment experts.
2. Mark Ainsley is the ______ of Little Meadow.
3. Miss Chambers ______ in Hill Road.
4. She is ______ a green **cardigan** when she opens the door.
5. The table in Mr Monks's kitchen has a lot of ______ on it.
6. There is a nervous ______ on Mr Monk's face when he talks about the dead men.

When Frank and Barry get back to the house, the mayor comes out to greet them. Today he is the picture of a country gentleman: tweed jacket, brown cord trousers and a thick cotton shirt with a green tie.
"Hello, gentlemen! Miss Robins tells me you have been to see Miss Chambers and Mr Monks. Could they help you at all?"
"They certainly made it clear how unpopular the three were in the village," answers Frank.
He looks hard at the mayor. Although he finds it hard to like this self-important little man, a gut feeling tells him that the mayor has nothing to do with the murders. The mayor looks a little uncomfortable when he sees Frank staring at him.

cardigan	Strickjacke
tweed	Wollstoff, Tweed
self-important	selbstgefällig
gut feeling	Bauchgefühl
to be miles away	mit den Gedanken ganz woanders sein
delighted	erfreut, entzückt
to bankrupt	(finanziell) ruinieren

Frank looks away. "Excuse me, Mr Ainsley. I was miles away for a moment. Do you have time to answer a few questions?"
The mayor's face relaxes and he straightens his back. "But of course, Detective Durham! I'd be delighted to help you in any way I can."

An hour and a half later, the two detectives come out of the mayor's office and walk through the house to the office at the back.
In the small office, the two detectives are silent for a few minutes. The mayor is a man who loves the sound of his own voice. He also knows about everything in the town. He told them that the "terrible three," as he called them, managed to bankrupt whole families.
"What surprises me," says Barry, "is that the three continued to live here after people began to find out what happened. Why didn't they look for new victims somewhere else?"

"Yes," agrees Frank and scratches his head. "Although the mayor said he didn't see them again after that article appeared in the local paper. That might be important. Can you phone Constable Jones, Mr Philips and Dr Sterling? Ask them if they remember when they last saw the three men alive."

Exercise 10: Unscramble the sentences. Bringen Sie die Wörter in die richtige Reihenfolge!

1. comes | the | greet | out | mayor | to | them

____

2. show | frustration | deep | his | wrinkles

____

3. Durham | not | like | Detective | the | mayor | very | much | does

____

____

4. finds | the | warfarin | Chambers's | Miss | detective | kitchen | in

____

____

5. bankrupt | whole | managed | families | they | to

____

Barry picks up the list of telephone numbers and walks over to the phone.

Frank stands by the window and thinks for a minute. Then he pulls out his mobile phone and rings the pathologist at the police station.

"Hi, Ann, it's Frank. Have you got a moment?"

"Sure, Frank. What's up?"

"How long does it take for rat poison to kill a rat?"

to scratch	kratzen
to depend on	abhängen von
hunch	(Vor-)Ahnung, Intuition

"That depends on the dose. Sometimes death can be very slow and painful if a rat doesn't eat much of the poison. Why do you ask?"

"Oh, just a little hunch of mine. I'll tell you about it when we get together[i] next week. Thanks again for your help."

"No problem. Always glad to help."

The line goes dead and Frank continues to look out of the window while Barry talks to the villagers.

Five minutes later, Barry puts down the phone. "Well, I've spoken to all of them. None of them remembers seeing the three after the newspaper article."

"And the article appeared in July sometime, didn't it?"

Barry picks up the photocopy of the newspaper article. "Yes, that's right."

"Which would mean about four weeks before Mr Edmonton died and about eight weeks before Michael Reed died."

"So? What's the connection?" Barry looks at Frank.

to get together bedeutet „sich treffen" und ist ein typisches **phrasal verb.** Es besteht also aus einem Verb *(to get)* und einem Partikel *(together)* und besitzt eine eigene Bedeutung. Weitere *phrasal verbs* mit *get* sind z.B.

to get about	herumkommen
to get at sb.	jmd. kritisieren
to get sth. down	etw. schlucken
to get up	aufstehen

He knows that expression. Frank knows something he doesn't.

to get one's skates on	ϟ ein bisschen dalli machen

"I think we should visit Mr Reed's house. I'm beginning to think these three little rats had to pay a lot for the cheese they stole. Ask Miss Robins to give us the key so we can go straight there tomorrow morning. Then we should get our skates on – otherwise we will be late for tea with Mrs Hutchinson!"

Exercise 11: Irregular verbs. Tragen Sie die Grundform der folgenden Verben ein!

1. told ______________________
2. stole ______________________
3. began ______________________
4. thought ______________________
5. knew ______________________
6. could ______________________

4 Tea and Biscuits at Home

It takes a while for Mrs Hutchinson to open the door. She smiles happily at the two detectives.
"Exactly on time. That is very good of you. I know how hard it is for people to be punctual these days. Come in, come in. Don't stand out in the cold. You can leave your shoes in the hall."
The two detectives smile at each other as they take off their shoes and then follow Mrs Hutchinson. A silver teapot and three cups and saucers are already on the table, next to a plate of biscuits.
In order not to be rude, Frank and Barry sit on either side of Mrs Hutchinson and accept a cup of rather watery tea and a biscuit.
"So young men, how are you getting on?" asks Mrs Hutchinson. "I know you have been to see my friends Miss Chambers and Mr Monks. Such nice people. Nasty business for both of them. I don't know how they could trust such horrible men."

nasty	scheußlich; gehässig
to trust	(ver)trauen
napkin	Serviette
to stir (sth.)	(etw.) (um)rühren
troublemaker	Unruhestifter

Frank picks up a biscuit. "Mr Monks said you never liked the three men. Perhaps you could tell us why that was?"
Mrs Hutchinson gives Frank a napkin and stirs her tea. "I worked as a teacher, so I recognize troublemakers immediately."
"You said you knew quite a lot about the three men," says Frank.

"Yes, I do. I like to do a bit of detective work myself," Mrs Hutchinson replies seriously, so that neither Barry nor Frank dare to smile.

"When I heard about their investment ideas, I realized they were up to no good. How can anyone sell life insurance to old people?" She sighs. "Of course, they took advantage of the people here. I tried to warn people, but it is difficult when you have no real proof."

to dare (to)	(etw.) wagen
to be up to no good	nichts Gutes im Schilde führen
to take advantage of	ausnutzen
proof	Beweis(e)
research	Recherche; Forschung
to blush	rot werden, erröten

She sighs again and sips her tea. "So, for a while, I did nothing, but when Mr Monks lost his job and then Nicholas Fields was so horrible to Miss Chambers, I knew it was time to do something. That's when I came up with the idea of going to the library in Norwich to do some research on the Internet."

Barry looks so surprised that Mrs Hutchinson laughs.

"I know. It is difficult to imagine someone like me on a computer. But there is a very nice girl at the library who taught me how to use the search engines. Now I always spend time on the Internet when I visit Norwich."

"And..." asks Frank, hoping that Mrs Hutchinson will get back to what she found out about the three men.

"It was there that I found a small piece about the scandal in Lowestoft. Not very much, but enough to want to know more. The following day I went to Lowestoft and visited the owner of the local paper. What a nice man. He had all the articles about the case on his computer. He printed them out for me and I took them straight to the mayor."

Barry takes yet another biscuit but blushes when he sees Mrs Hutchinson staring at him.

"Eat up, eat up, Detective Andrews. You look like a man who likes his food," she observes with a smile. "If you come tomorrow, I shall get a chocolate cake."
"What happened when the people in the village knew about the scandal in Lowestoft? Can you remember?" Frank asks.
She surprises him when she turns round quickly and for a second he sees what almost looks like anger in her bright blue eyes.

Die Verben **to remind** und **to remember** werden beide mit erinnern übersetzt und können daher leicht verwechselt werden. Sie werden jedoch in verschiedenen Zusammenhängen gebraucht:

to remember sb./sth.	sich an jmd./etw. erinnern
to remind sb. of sth.	jmd. an etw. erinnern

"Of course I can remember! I'm not senile! The young men didn't think they would have any problems with the people here – that we were all too polite to say anything to them. But they soon learnt differently. After a few days, they no longer did their food shopping at the supermarket. Michael Reed went away for two weeks and probably hoped everything would be forgotten when he got back."
"And what about the other two? Did they go away?" Frank holds his cup out for another cup of tea.
"No, they stayed here, although – as I said – no one really saw them in the village afterwards. You know, I rather hoped it was their guilty conscience that made them die. Don't you think that is possible, Detective Durham?"

guilty conscience	schlechtes Gewissen
to gasp	keuchen, nach Luft schnappen

"It might be, Mrs Hutchinson. But I believe someone poisoned the three men."
"Poisoned?" Mrs Hutchinson gasps. "How horrible! Do you have any idea who the murderer is?"
"I'm not really allowed to talk about our investigation with you, Mrs Hutchinson." Frank grins and shrugs his shoulders. "Almost every-

one in the village seems to have a good motive, except you, of course, Mrs Hutchinson!"
"Well, I'm VERY glad to hear it," says Mrs Hutchinson.

to grimace	das Gesicht verziehen
clue	Hinweis, Spur
pile	Stapel, Haufen

Ten minutes later, on their way back to Norwich in the car, Frank hits Barry playfully on the arm. "So, shall we go back for chocolate cake tomorrow? I'm sure Mrs Hutchinson would like to see you!"
Barry **grimaces**. "She reminds me of my history teacher. She used to look at me like that, too!"

At 10 a.m. the following morning, Frank and Barry are standing in front of Michael Reed's house when they see Mrs Hutchinson on the other side of the street. She waves and starts to cross the road.
"Good morning, you two. Have you got the keys for Mr Reed's house? Are you going to see if the murderer left any **clues**? Should I come in with you? I'm very good at finding clues, you know."
"That's very kind of you, Mrs Hutchinson, but I think it would be better if we worked on our own," answers Frank in a serious voice. "We can't let people say you solved the crime for us, can we?"
Mrs Hutchinson smiles. "I understand," she says. "But you will still be coming over later for tea, I hope."
Before either Frank or Barry can think of an excuse, Mrs Hutchinson turns and walks away.
"Oh great," mutters Frank. "We'll have to phone her later."
Barry shrugs his shoulders.
"We'd better go in, then, before anyone else invites us to tea." Frank turns the key in the lock and walks into the empty house.
There is a lot of post on the floor from the last few days and there is an even bigger **pile** of post on the table next to the door.
"One way not to pay your bills," Barry remarks.

They walk into the lounge. On the small coffee table is a TV magazine.

Frank looks at the date of the magazine. "This magazine is over four weeks old. Michael Reed probably bought it when he got back from his two-week trip away."

"That's a bit strange," comments Barry. "It is a weekly magazine, isn't it?"

"Yes, it is."

In the kitchen there is a strong smell of bad food. Barry opens the fridge and quickly closes it again.

"Yuk, that fridge is alive."

wardrobe	Kleiderschrank
rewind button	Rückspultaste
awful	furchtbar, schrecklich

Frank is puzzled. "He only died three days ago. The things in the fridge are much older. There is a pile of unopened post and a TV magazine that is four weeks old. I don't think Mr Reed was here between the time he got back from his trip and his death. So where was he?"

"But PC Jones says he found him here."

"Can you give him a call and ask him to come over for a few minutes? I think he lives in this street. I'll have a look upstairs."

Frank walks upstairs and into the bedroom. There is a suit on the wardrobe door. In the pocket he finds two tickets for a concert that took place three weeks ago. Next door, in the room Mr Reed obviously used as an office, Frank sees an answering machine. The tape is full. He presses the rewind button and listens to the messages. They are all over three weeks old.

He hears Barry open the door for PC Jones, so he walks downstairs, still puzzled.

"Where exactly did you find Mr Reed, Constable?" asks Frank.

"In his bed. Smelt and looked awful." The constable shudders.

"What did he have on?"

Exercise 12: Question tags. **Wie lautet der korrekte „question tag"?**

1. He reads a TV magazine, *doesn't he*?
2. He is an investment expert, ______________?
3. Detective Durham knows Mrs Hutchinson, ___________?
4. Michael Reed got back from his trip two weeks ago, ______________?
5. Mr Monks will find a job soon, ______________?
6. That would be nice, ______________?

"Some pyjamas. Really dirty they were, too," PC Jones replies.
"Did you find the other men, too?"
"Yes."
"What did they have on?" Frank asks.
"They were in pyjamas, too."
"What made you go to the houses each time?"
PC Jones thinks for a minute. "Miss Chambers told me about Nicholas Fields. She told me she went round to his house to get something back that belonged to her. When he didn't answer the bell or her calls, she decided to ask me to go round and check."
Frank scratches the back of his ear. "And Mr Edmonton?"
Again PC Jones pauses while he thinks. "That was Mr Monks. He said he couldn't get through to Mr Edmonton and was worried he might be hurt. And he also told me about Mr Reed."
"There is something VERY suspicious about those two," comments Frank, after the policeman has left.
"Yes," agrees Barry.

"Miss Chambers told us that Nicholas Fields sent her all her stuff back soon after she left the job at the architects. And I ran through Mr Reed's tape on the answering machine when I was upstairs, and I didn't hear one message from Mr Monks."

"Time to go and see them again..." Barry pulls on his jacket.

"This time with a search warrant," mutters Frank grimly.

As they leave the house, they see Mrs Hutchinson outside. She is speaking to PC Jones. She smiles at the constable when he says goodbye, but when she turns round she looks very worried. She leans on her stick and walks over to speak to Frank and Barry.

bell	Klingel, Glocke
search warrant	Durchsuchungs-befehl
grimly	grimmig, streng
whisper	Flüstern
to insist	beharren, bestehen auf
to humour sb.	jmd. seinen Willen lassen

Frank frowns. "Yes, Mrs Hutchinson, what is it?"

"I have found out something about Mr Monks and Miss Chambers that I think you should know," she says, almost in a whisper.

"Ah?" Frank's anger disappears immediately. "What is it?"

"I can't tell you here, you will have to come with me."

"One of us is going to have to go and pick up two search warrants at some point..." Frank looks hopefully at Barry who nods.

"Oh, but you'll come for a cup of tea first, won't you?" Mrs Hutchinson insists. "It is so important. I have bought a cake specially for you."

Better humour the woman, thinks Frank. It would be sad if she decided not to tell us what she knows.

Again the two detectives follow the tiny old lady into her house and then into the dining room. She goes out into the kitchen and comes back after five minutes with the silver tray, three cups and saucers, and a big chocolate cake.

envelope	Briefumschlag
sip	Schluck
old-fashioned	altmodisch
manners *pl*	Manieren, Benehmen
bad-tempered	schlecht gelaunt
to waste	verschwenden
to prove	beweisen
X-ray	Röntgenbild

"So what can you tell us, Mrs Hutchinson?" Frank asks as he takes a cup of tea from her.
He doesn't want Mr Monks or Miss Chambers to have a chance to escape.
"I've got the thing over here," Mrs Hutchinson says.
She walks over to a drawer and takes out an **envelope**. She brings it back to the table and sits down. With a little smile, she picks up her cup of tea and takes a **sip**.
"Exciting, isn't it?" she giggles.
Barry looks at her and smiles. Somehow he likes this funny woman with her **old-fashioned manners**. She makes such a nice change from the **bad-tempered** people in the town. He takes another bite of the chocolate cake and begins to feel very relaxed.
Frank, on the other hand, begins to feel impatient. They are **wasting** time. He sees Mrs Hutchinson watching him. She sniffs and looks a bit unhappy.
"Don't you like my tea and cake, Detective Durham?"
Frank sighs. "I am not a great cake fan, Mrs Hutchinson, but the tea is great."
To **prove** it, he swallows the rest of his tea and pushes his cup towards the teapot to show he wants another cup. Mrs Hutchinson smiles happily.
"That's a good boy. Now I'll show you what I have in this envelope," she says and pulls out two **X-rays** and a letter from a doctor.
"What have these got to do with the murder?" Frank asks puzzled.
"Oh, nothing at all," answers Mrs Hutchinson brightly. "But they are important for Miss Chambers and Mr Monks."
"I don't understand." Frank looks over at Barry to see if he has missed something.

But Barry is not really listening. He is holding his cake fork in one hand and is staring out of the window.
"Barry? Are you all right?"
Barry turns to Frank with a slightly dazed expression. "Sorry. I was sure I just saw Mr Monks and Miss Chambers at the window."
"Ah, perfect timing, as ever!" Mrs Hutchinson stands up. "Now you just sit there while I let them in. You can read this letter."
She puts the letter in front of Frank so he can read it easily. She tuts as she sees that Barry still has the cake fork in his hand.

dazed	benommen
to tut	sich mokieren
cancer	Krebs (Krankheit)
to stroke	streicheln, streichen über

"Let me put that down for you," she says, taking it out of his hand.
"This is all a bit weird," mutters Frank.
He reads the letter. "This is from the hospital in Norwich. Mrs Hutchinson went there for tests last month. She has cancer and this letter says there is nothing that the doctors can do about it."
"I'm not feeling very well," mutters Barry suddenly.
Frank sees that a white liquid is coming out of Barry's mouth.
Frank tries to stand up, but his legs don't seem to want to move. He looks at the tea and cake and realizes what has happened. Poison! He panics. Perhaps there is still a chance. He reaches very slowly into his pocket and manages to get his mobile phone. He presses 9-9-9 and slowly lifts the phone to his ear.
He hears the number beginning to ring, but before someone answers, a man's hand takes the phone out of his hand. Frank tries to turn his head to see who it is, but can't.
Mrs Hutchinson comes back into view. She looks at Frank sympathetically and gently strokes his hand.
"Now, now, Detective, we can't let you phone the police."
"I don't understand..." Frank mutters.

Exercise 13: Multiple choice. **Welcher Satz enthält die korrekte Übersetzung?**

1. Sie gibt ihm das Schreiben.
   a) ❒ She gives him the letter.
   b) ❒ She gives to him the letter.

2. Ich habe gestern einen Kuchen für Sie gebacken.
   a) ❒ I baked yesterday a cake for you.
   b) ❒ I baked a cake for you yesterday.

3. Sie erinnert Barry an sein Versprechen.
   a) ❒ She remembers Barry of his promise.
   b) ❒ She reminds Barry of his promise.

4. Barry fühlt sich nicht gut.
   a) ❒ Barry doesn't feel good.
   b) ❒ Barry doesn't feel well.

"Sit down for a moment, you two," Mrs Hutchinson says. "He has a right to know. It's going to take about another fifteen minutes anyway, after I drink my tea."

Frank watches as Mrs Hutchinson pours herself a large cup of tea from the pot.

"Now, you know what to do, don't you?" she asks and looks at the two people who are sitting next to Frank. "In a few minutes I won't be able to help you any more."

"Yes, of course, Mrs Hutchinson."

"We'll do everything exactly the way you told us, Mrs Hutchinson."

The voices belong to Miss Chambers and Mr Monks, Frank is sure, but he can't turn his head to see them.

to pour sb. sth.	jmd. etw. einschenken
to be asleep	schlafen
will	Testament; Wille
shame	Schande; Scham
bless him	*hier*: die gute Seele
I'm afraid (not)	leider (nicht)

"Good." Mrs Hutchinson picks up her cup and drinks the tea. When she finishes it, she gives a little sigh and turns back to look at Frank.

"It is all rather tragic really," she remarks and strokes Frank's hand again. "It was such a nice neighbourhood until those horrible men came to live here. There was no way that I could let the three of them get away with such bad behaviour. I have a big cellar here. It was perfect. There are no windows, so nobody can hear people inside. We put Mr Fields, Mr Edmonton and, later, Mr Reed down there and put rat poison in their drinks. Just a little at a time. We wanted them to be sorry, you see. They had been SO naughty!"

Mrs Hutchinson tidies her scarf and looks down the table at Barry, who looks as if he is asleep.

Mrs Hutchinson starts to fall forward. "Could you help me a bit, dears?" she asks.

Mr Monks and Miss Chambers come into view and carefully help Mrs Hutchinson back into the chair.

"Thank you," Mrs Hutchinson mutters and looks back at Frank.

"Anyway, to cut a long story short, we thought it would not be difficult to make it look as if I did the murders on my own. I am dying anyway, as you see from that letter. I've written a letter to say that I gave the men rat poison and put it with my will at the mayor's office. It's a shame the mayor listened to Dr Sterling."

Mrs Hutchinson sighs. "PC Jones, bless him, is not a problem, but I knew you would soon guess that the men did not die at home – and that is a problem. I can't allow anything else to happen to my two friends. So that, I'm afraid, is why we had to change our plans."

to confess	gestehen; beichten
bend	Kurve
to skid	schleudern, rutschen
to catch fire	Feuer fangen
madness	Wahnsinn

"Mr Monks has already phoned your police station to say that you are on the way to the station with me because I have confessed to the murders."

Frank looks at Mrs Hutchinson and tries to say something.

The old lady understands his question and shakes her head. "Oh no, they won't find the poison in your stomach, Detective Durham. Unfortunately, on the way to the police station, we will have a nasty car accident... on that bend between Southfield and Millwood. It is such a dangerous corner. Cars often skid off the road there. They catch fire and burn completely – and it is very difficult to identify the car after such an accident. There is never much left of the bodies... teeth, perhaps. But certainly nothing much for the pathologists..."

This is madness, Frank thinks. He is now finding it almost impossible to keep his eyes open.

Mrs Hutchinson smiles at him weakly. Then she slowly looks at Miss Chambers, who is putting the tea things on the tray.

"I think you can take Detective Durham's keys now, dear. He's almost gone. And by the time you bring the car back, we'll all be ready."

Murder in Battersea Park

Bernie Martin

1 The Murder

It is 6 a.m. and Constable Andrew Parker is jogging. Jogging is his hobby, and he runs through Battersea Park in London, which is just a couple of miles south of Marble Arch. He runs four days a week and likes to look at the black swans on the lake.

As he jogs past the playing area, he notices a young girl who is sitting on a bench with her head in her hands. He calls out and asks if she's okay, and she smiles at him and answers that she's just a bit tired.

constable	Polizist, Wachtmeister
to be (fast) asleep	(tief und fest) schlafen
to support	(unter)stützen
gently	sanft, zärtlich
to rest	(aus)ruhen

Satisfied, Andrew jogs on to the end of the park where he turns round and runs back the way he has come.

A few minutes later, as he is about to pass the bench on his way back, he sees the girl still sitting there. She is now leaning back on the bench and seems to be asleep. Andrew sees that her handbag has fallen to the ground. He smiles, jogs over and picks it up. As he puts the bag next to her on the bench, the girl's head falls to one side. Andrew puts his hands out to stop her from hurting herself. His hands support the back of her head, but she is getting heavier. He gently rests her head on the bench and feels that something is terribly wrong.

"Miss? Are you okay? Miss?"

She doesn't reply. Andrew realizes that the girl isn't asleep. He lets go of her head and starts to reach for her bag to find out who she is, when he notices that his hands are wet and **sticky**. In horror, he looks at the blood, then feels for a pulse – but there isn't one. He checks his watch, 6:14 a.m., then he takes out his mobile phone and calls his colleagues.

sticky	klebrig
to snore	schnarchen
bell	Klingel, Glocke
to mumble	murmeln, nuscheln
receiver	Telefonhörer; Empfänger
murder	Mord
body	*hier*: Leiche

At twenty past six, Detective Inspector Robert Kenny is fast asleep and **snoring**. He suddenly hears a **bell** ringing and reaches to the bedside table to switch the alarm clock off. His fingers find the button of the alarm clock, but the ringing continues. He hears his wife's voice **mumbling** in the dark.

"It's the telephone."

More awake now, he reaches over and lifts the **receiver**. "Hello?"

"Inspector Kenny?"

"Yes. Do you know what time it is?"

"Yes. Sorry, Inspector, but we have a **murder**."

Inspector Kenny wakes up very quickly. "Where?"

"In Battersea Park, sir."

"When?"

"About fifteen minutes ago. It was actually a constable who discovered the **body** while he was jogging. He's still there now."

"Right. I'm on my way. Can you inform Sergeant North?"

"That's next on my list, Inspector."

"Tell her to meet me in the park."

"I'll do that. Goodbye, Inspector."

Robert Kenny jumps out of bed and goes for a quick shower. As he is getting dressed, his wife Judith looks at him with sleepy eyes.

"Don't forget."

wedding anniversary	Hochzeitstag
sigh	Seufzer
to remind sb. (of sth.)	jmd. (an etw.) erinnern
curious	neugierig
to protect	(be)schützen

"What, Judith?"

"We are going to Alfredo's for our **wedding anniversary** at 7 p.m. this evening."

"Yes. Right. Of course."

Judith sits up in bed.

"You forgot, didn't you?"

"Of course not!"

Robert Kenny walks to the bed and gives Judith a kiss on the cheek. As he closes the bedroom door behind him, he lets out a deep **sigh**. "Thank God she **reminded me**!"

Exercise 1: Definitions. Enträtseln Sie die folgenden Definitionen!

gonggij | hebnc | bangadh | slupe | rones | roshew | revaniransy

1. Running to stay fit. ____________
2. You sit on this in a park. ____________
3. Ladies put their things in this. ____________
4. Feel this to see if someone's alive. ____________
5. Making a noise when asleep. ____________
6. Standing under water to wash. ____________
7. Celebrating your wedding day. ____________

Battersea Park is not far from Inspector Kenny's home and he arrives there at ten to seven. Two colleagues are keeping back the **curious** people behind tape which is **protecting** the scene of the

crime. Dr Jenkins, the police pathologist, is bent down and examining the body. Inspector Kenny goes to him and says good morning.
"Good morning, Inspector Kenny."
"Can you tell me anything yet, Dr Jenkins?"
"It was definitely murder. She was hit on the back of the head with a heavy object."

pathologist	Gerichtsmediziner
according to	laut, zufolge
to mutter	(vor sich hin) murmeln, brummeln
in charge (of)	zuständig (für); leiten
investigation	Ermittlung, Untersuchung

Inspector Kenny bends down to get a closer look.
"She looks very young."
"She's nineteen years old, according to her student's card. She died between six and six fifteen."
"How can you be so accurate? I hear that you are very good, Doctor, but you must be a real genius."
The doctor laughs. "Actually, Inspector, I'm not a genius. It's all thanks to your colleague."
"You mean the person who found the body?"
"Exactly. Constable Parker. He jogged past her at about 6 a.m. and when he came back at about six fifteen, she was dead."
"Is he still here?" Inspector Kenny asks.
"Yes. That's him over there, in the jogging suit standing under the large tree."
"Do you remember the name on the student's card, Doctor?"
"Yes. It's Linda Farraday. Your office is already checking on it."
"Great. Thanks very much."
"You're welcome, Inspector."
Inspector Kenny stands up and brushes the earth from the knee of his trousers. He walks across to Constable Parker, who is still standing under the tree, muttering to himself.
"Are you Constable Parker?"
"Yes, I am. I saw you talking to the doctor. Are you in charge of the investigation?"

witness	Zeuge
case	*hier*: Fall; Koffer
slim	schlank
stud	(Ohr-)Stecker

"That's right. My name's Inspector Robert Kenny. Now, tell me exactly what happened."

At that moment, Sergeant Kelly North, Inspector Kenny's assistant, arrives.

"Good morning, Inspector. Good morning, sir," she says, looking at Parker in his jogging clothes.

"Good morning, Sergeant. Could you take notes, please?"

"Certainly, Inspector."

"Sergeant, this is Constable Albert Parker..."

"Excuse me, sir. It's Andrew Parker."

"I'm sorry. This is Constable Andrew Parker. He's our main witness in this case. Now, Constable Parker, please tell us exactly what happened this morning."

Constable Parker tells them what happened. Kelly North looks him up and down, and she likes what she sees.

"Constable Parker? It seems strange that there was nobody in the park, even at 6 a.m."

"Well... When I was picking up the girl's handbag, I heard a noise behind the bushes. I turned around and saw a man running away."

Inspector Kenny looks up in interest.

"Can you describe him?"

"Yes, Inspector. He is quite tall and slim, about twenty-five years old. He has short dark hair and I seem to remember a silver stud in his left ear."

"That might help. Well done, Constable."

"Did you see anybody else?" Sergeant North asks.

"Well, actually, there was a lady who was walking her dog, but she was a long way away."

Inspector Kenny walks away, mobile phone to his ear, to call his station with the description. Kelly North looks at Parker with interest.

"Ever thought of joining the C.I.D.?"
"The Criminal Investigation Department is my dream, Sergeant."
"Well, why don't you fill in an application and send it to me?"
"I'll do that, Sergeant. Thank you very much."
"Don't mention it, Constable."
Sergeant North walks away with a smile on her face and goes over to Inspector Kenny, who is ready to leave.
"What were you talking to Parker about?" he asks.
"Oh, nothing, sir. Just small talk."
"Right. We need to go and see the girl's family."
Kelly's smile disappears. She nods grimly.
"Right, Inspector."

application	Bewerbung
Don't mention it!	Keine Ursache!; Nicht der Rede wert!
to nod	nicken
grimly	grimmig, streng

Exercise 2: Odd one out. Welches Wort ist das „schwarze Schaf"? Unterstreichen Sie das nicht in die Reihe passende Wort!

1. flat house apartment home
2. protect hit bang strike
3. walk jog run swim
4. mother father young aunt
5. tree flower bench cactus
6. jeans shirt pullover clothes
7. cat tiger dog lion

middle-aged	mittleren Alters
housekeeper	Haushälterin
I'm afraid (not)	leider (nicht), es tut mir leid, aber ...
matter	Sache, Angelegenheit
to show sb. in(to)	jmd. hereinführen
bookshelves *pl*	Bücherregale
Chippendale furniture	teure Möbelmarke aus dem 18. Jahrhundert
pin-striped suit	Nadelstreifenanzug

They drive to the address and find that it is a big house in a very expensive part of Chelsea. They go to the front door and it is answered by a **middle-aged** woman.

Inspector Kenny gives a little cough and gets ready to give the bad news.

"Mrs Farraday?"

"No, I'm Miss Dunbar, the **housekeeper**. How can I help you?"

"My name's Inspector Kenny and this is Sergeant North. We would like to speak to Mr and Mrs Farraday, please."

"That is not possible, **I'm afraid**."

"Why not?"

"Mrs Farraday died two years ago."

"I'm very sorry to hear that. Could we possibly speak to Mr Farraday?"

"Well, he's just about to leave for work."

"Miss Dunbar. This **matter** is very urgent. We're investigating and we need to speak to Mr Farraday."

"Oh! In that case, you should come in."

She **shows them into** a very large living room that is filled with **bookshelves** and **Chippendale furniture**. Miss Dunbar leaves to get Mr Farraday. The officers sit down, very carefully, on two chairs and wait.

A few minutes later, Mr Farraday enters the room. He is a tall, elegant middle-aged man and is dressed in a **pin-striped suit**.

"Good morning. You must be the people from the police. I hope it's not a problem with one of my patients?"

Inspector Kenny looks **confused**.
"Patients?"
"Yes. You see, I'm a doctor. My **surgery** is in Harley Street. I **treat** a lot of famous people and have many rock stars as patients."
"Now I see, Doctor. No, it's not one of your patients. It's your daughter, Linda."
"What is it this time? That girl is always getting into trouble. Have you **arrested** her?"
Inspector Kenny looks at the floor, and Kelly North **pretends** to be busy with her notes.
"I'm afraid I have some bad news for you, sir," Kenny finally says.
"Don't say it's drugs?"
"No, sir. Your daughter was murdered."
"Nooooo!" Dr Farraday shouts.
Suddenly the door opens and a young girl comes running into the room. She **hugs** Dr Farraday.
"Daddy, what's wrong?"
"It's Linda. These people are saying she was murdered."
The girl looks at Kelly North with a question in her eyes. The sergeant nods and the girl **bursts into tears**.
"Oh! No! It can't be true!"
She hugs her father harder, and they both cry into each other's shoulders.
After a few minutes, Dr Farraday stops crying and looks at Kenny and North.
"This is my daughter, Mandy. She is Linda's younger sister. What happened?"
"She was killed in Battersea Park," Sergeant North explains. "I'm sorry, sir... I know this isn't the right moment, but we have to get a

confused	verwirrt
surgery	*hier*: Arztpraxis; Chirurgie
to treat	behandeln
to arrest	verhaften
to pretend	vorgeben, vortäuschen
to hug sb.	jmd. umarmen
to burst into tears	in Tränen ausbrechen

morgue	Leichen-schauhaus

positive identification of the body as soon as possible. Could you and Mandy come with us to the morgue?"

"What? You want us to identify the body?"

"You can do it, sir. Mandy doesn't have to," the sergeant replies.

"Yes, all right. I need to (i) call my receptionist and cancel some appointments."

"That's fine, sir. We'll wait. We would also like to ask you both some questions at the station, after the morgue."

"Yes. I'll tell her to cancel all my appointments for today."

"What about my school, dad?"

"Yes, Mandy. Tell Miss Dunbar to ring them."

> Das Modalverb „müssen" kann im Englischen mit **must, need to** oder **have to** übersetzt werden.
>
> Während **must** darauf hindeutet, dass der Sprecher selbst etwas als notwendig empfindet, werden **need to** und **have to** verwendet, wenn die Verpflichtung von außen kommt oder eine allgemeine Tatsache zum Ausdruck gebracht werden soll.

2 The Questioning Begins

Exercise 3: Translation. **Lesen Sie weiter und unterstreichen Sie die Übersetzung der Wörter!**

Tochter   Tasse   sich entschuldigen   Nacht   wirken

They drive to the morgue, where Dr Farraday identifies his daughter Linda. Then they drive to the police station and all get a cup of tea.
Inspector Kenny takes Dr Farraday into an interview room.
"Dr Farraday. First let me apologize for putting you through all this."
"I know that you are just doing your job, Inspector."
"When was the last time you saw Linda, Dr Farraday?"
"Last night. She was leaving for her job at the disco."
"Do you know the name of the disco, sir?"
"Yes. It's the Starlight."
"What time was this?"
"About 9 p.m."
"Did she seem normal?"
"Normal! What's normal for a nineteen-year-old teenager?" Dr Farraday asks. "Actually, we had a little **argument**."
"What was it about, sir?"

argument	*hier*: Auseinandersetzung, Streit
medical studies	Medizinstudium
to adopt	adoptieren
pregnant	schwanger
upset	aufgeregt, verärgert
to settle sth.	etw. regeln

"The same as always. Linda broke off her **medical studies** and was working in that disco. She changed so much when her mother died," Dr Farraday replies.

"Yes. I'm sorry to hear that, sir," Inspector Kenny says calmly. "Please continue."

"Well, actually, Susan wasn't her real mother. We tried for years to have children but couldn't. Then we decided to **adopt**. Linda was only a baby when we got her."

"So Mandy is adopted too, sir?"

"Actually, no. We had Linda for about a year, then my wife Susan became **pregnant**."

"I see."

"To get back to last night, sir. So Linda left the house **upset**?" Inspector Kenny asks.

"Well, not really. We agreed that Linda would give up her job at the disco and that she would continue her medical studies in New Zealand next month."

"So everything was **settled** then?"

"Yes. At least I thought it was," Dr Farraday replies.

In another room, Kelly North is interviewing Mandy Farraday.

"When was the last time you saw your sister, Mandy?" the sergeant begins.

"Yesterday evening as she was leaving for work," Mandy replies, playing with a ring on her right hand.

"Did Linda seem upset or worried?"

"No. Linda loved her job at the disco."

"Where did she work?"

"The Starlight Disco."

"So, how did you get on with your sister?" the sergeant asks Mandy.

"We got on well. I mean we fought sometimes, but I don't know any sisters that don't."

"Yes, of course," Sergeant North agrees. "I must say, you and Linda didn't look like sisters."

"That's because we weren't. Linda was adopted, you know?"

"I didn't know that."

"Oh yes. I'm daddy's only real child. I'm going to study medicine and become a doctor like him. He'll be so proud of me."

"Mandy, can you think of anyone who would want to kill your sister?"

"No. Everyone loved Linda. She was always the centre of attention."

"Do you have any idea why Linda was in Battersea Park at six in the morning?"

"She usually finished work at about 4 a.m.," Mandy replies and shrugs. "I suppose she went to the park for some fresh air before going home."

"Well. That's about all for now. I'll call you if I need to speak to you again."

Back in their office, Inspector Kenny looks at the clock on the wall and sees that it's nearly half past twelve.

"Let's go to the canteen for lunch, Kelly."

"Good idea, Robert. I'm starving."

Kenny and North discuss the case over lunch. They decide to visit the Starlight Disco that afternoon.

to get on (with sb.)	(mit jmd.) auskommen
proud	stolz
centre of attention	Zentrum der Aufmerksamkeit
to shrug (one's shoulders)	die Achseln zucken
to suppose	annehmen, vermuten
That's all for now.	Das war's fürs Erste.
to starve	(ver)hungern

Exercise 4: Fill in the blanks. **Lesen Sie weiter und fügen Sie die Übersetzung der angegebenen Wörter ein!**

When they arrive there, the disco is **1.** leer ______________, but there is a young **2.** Frau ______________ behind the bar who is polishing glasses. She is about twenty-five years old, rather **plump** and she is wearing too much make-up.
"Sorry. We don't **3.** aufmachen ______________ until this evening."
North and Kenny take out and **4.** zeigen ______________ their **identity cards**.
"Oh! You're the police. I suppose you've come to **5.** fragen ______________ about Linda?"

"That's right," Kelly North replies and takes out her notebook. "How do you know about Linda? The information hasn't been **released** to the press yet."
"Dr Farraday called about half an hour ago to tell us that Linda was killed this morning."
Tears fill her eyes and she takes a **tissue** out of her handbag.
"We got on really well, you know."

plump	mollig
identity card	(Dienst-)Ausweis
to release	freigeben, freilassen
tissue	Papiertaschentuch

"Could you give me your name, please?"
"Oh! Sure, sorry. I'm Sandra Williams. Linda and I worked together most of the time," the woman answers.

"When was the last time you saw Linda, Ms Williams?"
"This morning. We did the late shift and finished just after five in the morning."
"Did you leave together?"
"No. Linda said she needed to talk to Ned. She seemed very excited about something."
"Do you know what she was excited about?"
"No, I'm sorry. I don't. I did ask, but Linda said she'd tell me this evening."
Inspector Kenny is busy studying the photographs of the table dancers. Suddenly a door at the back of the disco opens and a tall man enters.

late shift	Spätschicht
to match	passen zu; vergleichen
to back off	zurückgehen, zurückweichen
to clear sth. up	etw. (auf)klären

"What's going on here? I'm afraid I must ask you to leave."
Inspector Kenny walks across the room to him, and while he does, he remembers Constable Parker's description:
"He is tall, slim with short dark hair, wearing a silver stud in his left ear."
The description matches perfectly. Inspector Kenny shows the man his identity card.
"Inspector Kenny, C.I.D."
The man backs off a step. "Police, here in my club. What do you want?"
Kenny continues: "Let me clear something up. I'm the one who asks the questions. Have you got that?"
"Uhmm. Yes, Officer."
"Now. Who are you and what are you doing here?"
"My name's Ned Taylor and I'm the owner of this club."
"Very good, Mr Taylor. I think you heard about Linda Farraday, didn't you?"

"Yes, of course. Terrible thing," Mr Taylor replies.
"Mr Taylor, where were you at 6 a.m. this morning?"
"I was at home. I was getting ready for bed."
"Are you sure, Mr Taylor?" Inspector Kenny asks.
"Of course I'm sure."
"Mr Ned Taylor, I'm arresting you on suspicion of murdering Linda Farraday!"
Ned Taylor and Sandra Williams look up in shock as Inspector Kenny closes the handcuffs on Taylor's wrists. The inspector looks across at Sandra Williams.

suspicion	Verdacht
handcuffs *pl*	Handschellen
to hesitate	zögern
to wave (one's hands)	winken; schwenken
duty sergeant	diensthabender Polizist
to interrogate	befragen, verhören

"Ms Williams. I would like you to come to the station, too. We have more questions for you."
Sandra Williams hesitates. "What about the club?"
Ned Taylor waves his handcuffed hands at her.
"Sandra, just lock up and come with us. Okay?"
"If you say so, Ned."
She gets her handbag and as they leave the club, she locks up behind her.

When they arrive at the station, the officers hand Ned Taylor over to the duty sergeant, who puts him in a cell. Another officer takes Sandra Williams to an interview room. Kelly North gets her a cup of tea and biscuits and tells her that she will be back very soon. She then goes to Inspector Kenny's office.
"There you are, Kelly. What do you think?"
"You quite surprised me when you arrested Taylor, Robert."
"Why? You know Constable Parker saw someone in the park this morning who fits his description."

"It just seems too easy. Maybe he wasn't the only one in the park."
"You could be right, Kelly. I'm hoping that by putting Ned Taylor in a cell, he will be scared enough to tell the truth."
"Good idea, Robert."
"Look. Let's interrogate Williams together first. You might hear something I don't. After that we'll do Taylor."
"Okay, you're the boss."
They go to the interview room where Sandra Williams is waiting for them. They sit down opposite her and Inspector Kenny starts the interrogation.

Exercise 5: Questions about the text. Beantworten Sie folgende Fragen zum Text!

1. Where was Mr Taylor at 6 a.m. this morning?

   ____

2. What is the name of Inspector Kenny's assistant?

   ____

3. What is the name of the murdered girl?

   ____

4. What is Mr Taylor's disco called?

   ____

5. What does Mr Taylor wear in his left ear?

   ____

to look forward to	sich freuen auf
for a change	zur Abwechslung
prisoner	Gefangener
objection	Einwand, Einspruch

"Right, Ms Williams. You told Sergeant North that you last saw Linda Farraday just after five this morning. Is that correct?"

"Yes, that's right, Inspector," Sandra Williams replies.

"How was your working relationship with Ms Farraday?"

"Very good."

"What about your boss, Ned Taylor?"

"Well. He's a difficult man to work for but very fair. Of course, Linda got on with him better than I did."

"Why do you say that?"

"Don't you know? They were lovers!"

Inspector Kenny and Sergeant North look at each other in surprise.

"Do you know her family?"

"Well, I met Dr Farraday once. A real gentleman."

"What about her sister?"

"You mean Mandy. Oh yes, I know her. I don't think that she's a very nice person."

"So you don't like her?"

"Nobody I know does. Especially Linda," Sandra Williams answers.

"Why?"

"She was always reminding Linda that she was adopted. She was often telling lies about Linda, trying to get her into trouble."

"So Linda and Mandy didn't get on, then?"

"Not at all. Linda only tried to get on with Mandy because of her father. She was looking forward to going to New Zealand."

"One last question, Ms Willams. Do you think Ned Taylor could have killed Linda?"

Sandra Williams looks shocked and does not reply immediately.

"No. No, I don't think so," she then says. "He always plays the hard man, but I don't think he would kill someone."

"Well, thank you very much, Ms Williams. You were a big help."
"Should I go and open the club now?"
"Yes, if you wish. Goodbye."

Exercise 6: Correct the mistakes. Lesen Sie weiter und unterstreichen Sie die zehn Fehler. Verbessern Sie sie!

Robert Kenny and Kelly North take her to the door and ask the duty sergeant to brought Ned Taylor to the inter view room.
"Kelly, wen we interrogate Taylor, do you want to be the good guy or the baad guy?"
"Let me be the good guy **for a change**. You playt the good guy last week."
"Okay, here he come."
Ned Taylor is led in and sits on the chair opposite thems. Kelly North smiles at him. "Mr Taylor. Would you like a kup of tea?"
Robert Kenny interrupts rudely. "No tea for the **prisoner**, Sergeant!"
"Fery well, Inspector. Now, Mr Taylor, do you have ani **objection** to us recording this interview?"

1. ____________________ 6. ____________________

2. ____________________ 7. ____________________

3. ____________________ 8. ____________________

4. ____________________ 9. ____________________

5. ____________________ 10. ____________________

"No." Mr Taylor is obviously nervous.
"Could you please state your full name for the record?"
"Edward Nigel Taylor."
"But you're known as 'Ned', aren't you?" Kelly North asks very politely.

obviously	offensichtlich
to state	angeben; feststellen
for the record	für das Protokoll
to mess sb. about	jmd. an der Nase herumführen
tray	Tablett
intently	intensiv, durchdringend
to stare	starren
to whisper	flüstern

"Yes, that's right," Taylor replies nervously.
"Please state your address, Mr Taylor."
"It's 31 Highbury Road, Chelsea."
Robert Kenny leans over angrily. "Don't mess us about, Sonny. Give us the postcode as well."
Taylor looks scared. "Er, sorry. It's SW6 1HS."
Kelly North smiles sweetly.
"Thank you very much, Mr Taylor."
"You're welcome, Officer."
There is a knock at the door and Constable Parker enters, carrying a tray. He gives Ned Taylor a cup and looks intently at his face.
Ned Taylor is obviously uncomfortable. "Tell him to stop staring at me."
Constable Parker walks round the table and puts a cup of tea in front of Inspector Kenny.
As he does this, he whispers in Kenny's ear. "It's him, Inspector. One hundred per cent."
"Thank you, Constable. You may leave now."
Kelly North shakes her head in amused surprise. Robert Kenny continues to play the bad guy.
"So, Ned, why did you kill Linda Farraday?"
"What!" He jumps to his feet. "I didn't kill her."

Exercise 7: Match up the synonyms. Ordnen Sie die Synonyme den Begriffen links zu!

1. ☐ state	a) bang, strike, hit
2. ☐ nervous	b) mug, pot, glass
3. ☐ scared	c) go, depart, exit
4. ☐ cup	d) say, report, inform
5. ☐ stop	e) halt, cease, finish
6. ☐ knock	f) afraid, terrified, fearful
7. ☐ leave	g) worried, anxious, upset

Inspector Kenny leans over the table and quickly pushes Ned back onto the chair. Kelly North shakes her head.

"Sir, I must protest..."

Inspector Kenny turns to her and winks [i] but shouts angrily, "Sergeant North! I am your direct superior. Take your notes, but let me handle this."

Vorsicht vor falschen Freunden!

to wink	zwinkern
to wave	winken

Kelly North pretends to be upset.

"Yes, sir."

"Now then, Taylor. Why did you lie to me?"

"What! When? I mean."

"In your club you told me that you were at home at six this morning. Before you lie again, we have a witness who saw you in Battersea Park at that time."

to wink	zwinkern
superior	Vorgesetzter
let me handle this	lass/lassen Sie mich das in die Hand nehmen

in defeat	niedergeschlagen
ϟ to come down a bit	ϟ runterkommen
direction	Richtung
yard	Längenmaß: 91 cm
to blame sb. (for sth.)	jmd. beschuldigen, jmd. die Schuld an etw. geben

"Well, your witness must be lying."

"Mr Taylor. Our witness is a policeman. I am giving you one last chance. Either you tell us everything, or I'll put you back in the cell and throw away the key."

Ned Taylor hangs his head in defeat.

"Okay. I admit I lied," he says quietly.

"So why don't you tell the truth for a change?"

"Yes, I was in the park at six this morning. When she was finishing work, Linda told me that she was expecting my baby."

"How did you react?"

"Badly, I'm afraid. I was shocked. Anyway, we started to have an argument, but Linda was scared Sandra would hear."

"So you arranged to meet in the park?"

"Yes. We often went there after work to come down a bit."

"What happened exactly, Mr Taylor?"

"I was a bit late. I saw a woman walking a dog and a jogger who was running in the other direction. I came round the corner and walked to the bench from behind."

"Why from behind?"

"Well, it was one of our games. I would cover her eyes with my hands and Linda would have to guess who it was."

"I see. So did she guess it was you?"

"No. I got to within a few yards and saw that she was half lying on the bench. Then I saw the blood on the back of her head and panicked."

"So you ran away?"

"I'm not proud of it, but yes. I saw the jogger coming back and knew that I would get blamed for the murder. So I ran."

"Are you sure you are telling the truth, Mr Taylor?"
"I swear, Inspector. I loved Linda. I was going to ask her to marry me. She was expecting my child!"
"Right, Mr Taylor. That's all for now. I'm afraid you have to go back to your cell for the time being.(i)"
"Anything you say, Inspector. Honestly, I am not the murderer."

escort	Eskorte, Geleitschutz
shame	Schande; Scham
to bet	wetten

Inspector Kenny rings for an escort, and a constable takes Ned Taylor back to his cell. Kenny turns to Sergeant North.
"So, Kelly. What do you think?"
"Well. It certainly looks as though Ned Taylor is the killer. What can his motive be?" the sergeant replies.
"I don't know. Maybe he didn't want to marry her. I'm sure that will become clear soon enough."
"I don't know, Robert. It all seems too easy."
"What do you mean?" the inspector asks.
"Well. Ned Taylor in the park. I think it could be any of them. Dr Farraday, Mandy, or even Sandra Williams."

Die Wendung **for the time being** bedeutet „vorläufig", „vorerst".

"What motive could her father have?"
"Dr Farraday is a very conservative man. The shame was too much for him, perhaps," Sergeant North replies.
"What about Mandy Farraday? Surely you don't think it was her?"
"Maybe!"
"But she's only seventeen," Inspector Kenny states.
"You heard what Sandra Williams said about Mandy and Linda not liking each other."
"So you think one of them is lying?"
"I do, and I'm betting it's Mandy."
"How about this, Kelly? Sandra Williams is in love with Ned Taylor.

She overhears Linda telling Ned that she is pregnant and wants him to marry her. Sandra follows Linda to Battersea Park and kills her in a jealous rage?"
"Also possible, Robert. So, what do we do now?"
"What do you suggest, Kelly?"
"Maybe we should question them all again?"

to overhear	zufällig (mit)-hören
jealous (of)	eifersüchtig (auf), neidisch (auf)
rage	Wut(anfall); Zorn
to question sb.	jmd. befragen

Exercise 8: Unscramble the sentences. Bringen Sie die Wörter in die richtige Reihenfolge!

1. the am I murderer not

___

2. woman saw I dog a walking a

___

3. my was she child expecting

___

4. be motive his what can ?

___

5. too seems easy it all

___

"You're right, Kelly," Robert Kenny replies. "Let's question them all again tomorrow. I must run now. If I'm not on time for our anniversary dinner, my wife will kill me."

"Congratulations, Robert," she smiles. "Which one is it?"
Robert Kenny thinks for a while.
He jumps when the telephone next to his elbow rings.
"Robert Kenny speaking?"
"Dr Jenkins here. We spoke at the crime scene in Battersea Park this morning."
"Yes, Doctor. Just let me switch you to the loudspeaker. My colleague should hear this, too. Okay, go ahead."

to jump	*hier*: erschrecken, zusammenzucken
crime scene	Tatort
to receive	erhalten; empfangen
severe	heftig; streng
blow	Schlag

"Right. Linda Farraday died after receiving a severe blow to the back of the head. After you left, we found a heavy tree branch, in the bushes behind the body. There was blood on it, so we took it to the laboratory with us. We tested it and discovered that it is definitely the murder weapon."
"Are there any fingerprints on the branch, Doctor?"
"I'm afraid not. Sorry," Dr Jenkins replies.
"Thanks very much–"
"Oh, Inspector. There's one more thing."
"Yes, Doctor?"
"Linda Farraday was about ten weeks' pregnant."
"That's a big help. Thanks very much, Dr Jenkins. Goodbye."
Inspector Kenny hangs up and starts to put his jacket on.
"So, Robert. How many years have you been married?"
"You know, Kelly, I really can't say. Eleven, I think."
Kelly North smiles and reaches for her coat.

3 Turning Up the Heat

The next morning they interrogate Dr Farraday first. Inspector Kenny greets him politely.

"Good morning, Dr Farraday. We are really sorry to bother you again."

"No problem. I know you're only doing your job. Besides, I want Linda's killer caught."

"Exactly. We only have a few questions for you, Doctor."

to bother sb.	jmd. belästigen
besides	außerdem
recently	kürzlich, jüngst

"Ask anything you like."

"Mandy told us yesterday that she and Linda got on well, but Sandra Williams says it was the opposite."

"Who is Sandra Williams?"

"She's Linda's colleague. They worked together at the Starlight disco."

"Oh, I see. Well, to be perfectly honest, I'm not too sure. You see, I work long hours and haven't seen too much of my girls recently. You'll have to ask Miss Dunbar, my housekeeper. She saw them more often than me."

"What's your feeling, Doctor? Did they get on well?"

"Of course they argued a lot, like most sisters. I sometimes had the feeling that Mandy was jealous of Linda."

"What do you mean?"

"Well. Little things, really. Mandy always blamed Linda if anything went wrong. Linda's favourite clothes would disappear and Miss

Dunbar would find them in the back of Mandy's wardrobe. Of course, Mandy would say that Linda did it herself to get her into trouble," Dr Farraday sighs and shakes his head.

wardrobe	Kleiderschrank
to sigh	seufzen
How dare you!	Wie können Sie es wagen!
to raise sb.	*hier*: jmd. großziehen; jmd. wecken

"Thank you, Dr Farraday. Now, one last question. Where were you at 6 a.m. yesterday morning?"
Dr Farraday gets upset.
"How dare you! Do you honestly think I killed my own daughter?"
"Adopted daughter, Dr Farraday."
"I raised that girl as my own. My wife, too. I loved her just as much as Mandy."
"Please just answer the question, Doctor."
"I was in bed. Where else would I be at six in the morning?"
"Thank you for your help, Doctor. That's all for now."

Exercise 9: Prepositions. Füllen Sie die Lücken der folgenden Sätze mit den Präpositionen on, at oder in!

1. The alarm rang early ______ the morning.
2. It was cold ______ the park.
3. Linda and Mandy didn't get ______ well.
4. Kelly met Robert ______ the station.
5. Dr Farraday works long hours ______ his surgery.
6. ______ 6 a.m., I was ______ bed.

to fumble	herumtasten
to make a big deal of sth.	viel Wind um etw. machen

The next person to come in is Sandra Williams.
"Good morning, Ms Williams. Please take a seat."
She sits down and starts fumbling in her handbag. Kelly North leans over to her.
"What's the problem, Ms Williams? Are you looking for something?"
"No. Yes. I can't find my tissues."
Kelly stands up and gets a box of tissues from a sideboard.
"Here, use these."
"Oh, thank you, Miss. You are so kind."
"No problem, Ms Williams. Now then, we have a few more questions for you."
"Okay."
"You told us yesterday that Linda and Mandy didn't get on. Is this true?"
"Of course. Why should I lie? Linda just didn't make a big deal of it out of respect for her father."
"Do you think Mandy killed her sister?"
"Oh, my God. You can't believe...? No. I know Mandy hated Linda, but kill her...?"
"Hate is a very strong word, Ms Williams."
"Well, Mandy did hate her! Wouldn't you if your sister stole your boyfriend?"
Kelly North leans back in surprise.
"Could you say that again?"
"What? I thought you knew. When Linda started to work at the Starlight, Mandy came with her. Anyway, she fell in love with Ned and they started seeing each other."
"So what happened then?"
"Well, about six months ago, Ned finished with Mandy and started seeing Linda. There were explosions, I can tell you!"
"Did you have a relationship with Mr Taylor?"

ϟ to fancy sb.	ϟ auf jmd. stehen
confirmation	Bestätigung

"No. I mean, I fancy him, but he's not interested in me."
"Okay, Ms Williams. Oh, one more thing. Where were you at six yesterday morning?"
"I went straight home from the club. No, wait. On my way home, I stopped at the bakery at the end of my street. I had to wait a few minutes, because they don't open until six."
"What's the name of the bakery and the street, Ms Williams?"
"Crofts. I think it's number 43, Henshall Avenue."
"Right. We'll check that. Thank you very much, Ms Williams."

Robert Kenny looks in the phone book and calls the bakery while they are waiting for Ned Taylor. He speaks to the baker's wife and describes Sandra Williams. The baker's wife knows Sandra quite well and Inspector Kenny receives confirmation that she was there at six the day before.
Ned Taylor enters the room still in handcuffs. The police escort sits him in the chair opposite North and Kenny, nods and leaves.
Inspector Kenny looks at Taylor for a long time without saying anything. Ned Taylor becomes more and more nervous. Finally, Robert Kenny leans back in his chair.
"Mr Taylor. Why didn't you tell us about Mandy yesterday?"
"Mandy Farraday? Well, I didn't think it was important."
"How about letting us decide what's important, Mr Taylor? Tell us about Mandy."
"Well. She sort of forced the relationship on me. She's young and I thought it would be good for my ego, you know?"
"No. I don't know, Mr Taylor."
"Sandra did warn me that Mandy only wanted to go out with me because Linda fancied me. I didn't believe her then, but now I'm not so sure."
"So you finished with Mandy to go out with Linda?"

demanding	fordernd, anspruchsvoll
to sulk	schmollen
to accuse sb.	jmd. beschuldigen
to cheat (on sb.)	(jmd.) betrügen

"Not really. Mandy was always demanding. If she didn't get her way, she would sulk, as schoolgirls do."

"So you finished with her?" the inspector asks.

"Yes. I finished with her. She flew into a rage and accused me of cheating on her with Linda, but it wasn't like that. Linda and I didn't start seeing each other until a week later."

"So, Mandy accepted it in the end?"

Exercise 10: Translations quiz. Übersetzen Sie und enträtseln Sie das Lösungswort!

1. sicher _ _ □ _
2. sprechen _ _ _ □ _
3. wirklich (Adv.) □ _ _ _ _ _
4. Mädchen _ _ □ _
5. später _ □ _ _ _
6. entscheiden □ _ _ _ _ _
7. verlassen _ _ □ _ _
8. gestern □ _ _ _ _ _ _ _ _

Lösung: □□□□□□□□

"Not really. She threatens me constantly. She tried to get me in trouble with the tax office a few times and spread nasty gossip about me. About Linda, too, as far as I know."

"Do you think Mandy killed Linda?"

"No way! [i] Mandy can be a little minx at times, but I can't believe she would kill her sister."

to threaten	(be)drohen
tax office	Finanzamt
to spread	(sich) verbreiten
nasty	scheußlich; gehässig
gossip	Tratsch, Klatsch
⚡ minx	⚡ freches Ding, Zicke

Die umgangssprachliche Wendung **No way!** übersetzt man mit „Auf keinen Fall!" oder „Ich glaub's nicht!"

There's no way we can afford this.
Das können wir uns auf keinen Fall leisten.

"Right, Mr Taylor. You can go home now."

"What? Really? I can go home?"

"Yes, but let us know where you are at all times. We might have to speak to you again."

"Yes, Inspector. I'll do that, and thanks."

Ned Taylor leaves the room very quickly.

4 The Killer Is Caught

Kelly North looks at Robert Kenny in surprise. "Why are you letting him go, Robert?"

"Because Ned Taylor is not the killer."

"Well. Who is it then?"

"I'll tell you when I'm one hundred per cent sure," Inspector Kenny replies.

"Oh! I hate it when you do that."

"Kelly, trust me."

"Well there's only Mandy left to question now. Should I call her in, Robert?"

"Not yet, Kelly. I want to make a quick phone call first," the inspector replies thoughtfully.

He takes Dr Farraday's business card out of his wallet and dials the number. He covers the mouthpiece and tells Sergeant North that he's putting the call on loudspeaker so that she can hear, too.

"Hello, Farraday residence. Miss Dunbar speaking?"

"Hello, Miss Dunbar. This is Inspector Kenny. We met yesterday."

"Yes, I remember, Inspector. What can I do for you?" the housekeeper asks.

"Well, Miss Dunbar. I'm just calling to confirm that Dr Farraday was in the house at 6 a.m. yesterday morning."

to trust	(ver)trauen
thoughtfully	nachdenklich
wallet	Brieftasche
to dial	wählen (Telefon)
to confirm	bestätigen

the night before last	vorgestern Abend

"He was, Inspector. He came down for breakfast at half past six, as always. He finished just before you arrived."
"I see. What about Mandy? What time does she usually have breakfast?"
"She usually comes down just after Dr Farraday."
"And yesterday?"
"Oh, she didn't have breakfast yesterday. She came home about ten minutes before you arrived."
"Are you sure, Miss Dunbar?" Inspector Kenny asks.
"Yes. You see, it was a full moon the night before last and I could not sleep," the houskeeper explains. "Anyway, I got up at about half past four to get a glass of water. Then I heard the front door closing and looked out of my bedroom window. That's when I saw Mandy walking towards town."
"Did she say where she went?"
"No, she didn't."
"Another question, Miss Dunbar. Did Mandy and Linda get on with each other?"
"They did before Mrs Farraday died. Then, Mandy changed. She was always telling Linda that she wasn't part of the family. Terrible thing, really."
"How was their relationship during the last few months?" Inspector Kenny asks.
"To be perfectly honest, Inspector, it went from bad to worse," the housekeeper sighs.
"Thank you, Miss Dunbar. That is a big help. Goodbye."
"Goodbye, Inspector."
Robert Kenny puts the phone down and turns to Kelly North.
"Mandy is the killer, Kelly. I'm sure of it."
"You could be right, Robert, but I still think it was Ned Taylor."

to prove	beweisen
to take over	übernehmen, ablösen
to pat	*hier:* (Haare) zurechtstreichen; tätscheln
to sneer	spöttisch lächeln

"Yes, that's also possible. However, I can't see him killing his girlfriend because she was pregnant and wanted to marry him."
Inspector Kenny shakes his head.
"Well, if it is Mandy, how do we prove it? We have no fingerprints on the branch, nobody believes that she could murder anyone, and nobody saw her at the scene of the crime."
"I have an idea. Call her in now."
Sergeant Kelly North opens the door and calls Mandy Farraday into the interview room.
Inspector Robert Kenny decides to do the questioning.
"Hello, Mandy. May I call you Mandy?"
Mandy smiles at him shyly.
"If you want to, Inspector. Are you married?"
Inspector Kenny goes red and looks at Kelly North for help.
Sergeant Kelly North takes over.
"Mandy. I'll ask the questions, if you don't mind?"
Mandy Farraday pats her hair and smiles again at Inspector Kenny.
"Mandy? You told us yesterday that you and your sister Linda got on quite well?"
Mandy smiles again, still looking at Robert Kenny.
"Yes, I did. I mean sometimes we argued, but nothing that most sisters don't do."
"I see. Well, Sandra Williams and Miss Dunbar see it differently."
Mandy looks at Kelly North for the first time and sneers.
"Sandra Williams and Miss Dunbar! What do they know? They have no idea what life is about."
"Why do you say that?"

Exercise 11: Multiple choice. Vervollständigen Sie die Aussagen zur Geschichte!

1. When Kenny and North entered the disco, ________________.
   a) ❒ they were given a drink
   b) ❒ they were asked to leave
   c) ❒ Kenny banged his head

2. Battersea Park's lake has ________________.
   a) ❒ black swans
   b) ❒ white geese
   c) ❒ black ducks

3. Miss Dunbar got up at half past four to ________________.
   a) ❒ go to the bathroom
   b) ❒ get a glass of water
   c) ❒ get a cup of coffee

4. Linda wanted to study in ________________.
   a) ❒ Australia
   b) ❒ Great Britain
   c) ❒ New Zealand

5. Sandra Williams is Linda's ________________.
   a) ❒ cousin
   b) ❒ sister
   c) ❒ colleague

"Miss Dunbar is just a slave," Mandy continues. "She never married and never has fun. She's just a dried-up old spinster."

"And Sandra Williams?"

"Oh, she's not worth talking about. She's uneducated and I know that she's secretly in love with Ned Taylor. She's just too stupid to do anything about it. She and Linda were always making plans to get me into trouble."

"So, you and Linda fought a lot?"

"Well, yes, but it doesn't mean I killed her."

"Who do you think killed Linda?"

"Ned Taylor, of course. He's terrified he'll lose his freedom. He wants to have fun, not be married."

"We were informed that you and Linda started fighting a lot after Mrs Farraday died."

slave	Sklave/Sklavin
ϟ spinster	(alte) Jungfer
uneducated	ungebildet
to be terrified	panische Angst haben
to pinch	zwicken
to cause	verursachen
stiff	steif

"That's right. It was all Linda's fault, you know."

"What was Linda's fault?"

"Mum's death!"

"Did Linda kill her?" Sergeant North sounds surprised.

"Not directly. Mum picked us up from school one day. Linda started a fight with me and started pinching me."

"What happened then?"

"I screamed and Mum turned round to tell us off. She didn't see another car coming out of a side street and we crashed right into it."

"Mandy, surely it was your scream that caused the accident?"

Mandy's body goes stiff and she starts to shout.

"I'm telling you it was Linda's fault! It was always Linda's fault! I'm daddy's good little girl."

Robert Kenny looks at Kelly North and gestures for her to take it easy.
"Okay, Mandy. We can see you're upset. Let's take a short break. Would you like something to drink?"
"A coke, please. I'm hungry, too."

Exercise 12: In other words. Welche Wörter stehen miteinander in Zusammenhang? Ordnen Sie zu!

1. ☐ scream	a) bang
2. ☐ stiff	b) assist
3. ☐ inform	c) pause
4. ☐ help	d) shout
5. ☐ stupid	e) tell
6. ☐ crash	f) silly
7. ☐ stop	g) hard

Kelly North rings for a woman police constable to bring a coke and a sandwich. When she arrives, North and Kenny walk to the coffee machine in the hall.
"She's a handful, isn't she, Kelly?"
"She certainly is. How can she flirt and eat, when her sister died yesterday?" the sergeant shakes her head.

to be a handful	schwierig sein
obsessed	besessen

"Good question. Do you think she's a little crazy?"
"Either crazy – or obsessed. She's seventeen, but she acts as if she's ten."

"Yes, you're right."
They walk back to the interview room and Kelly North continues the questioning.
"Mandy. Did you go to school yesterday?"
"I wanted to, but my father said I shouldn't."
"Didn't you care that your sister was dead?"
"Not really."
Robert Kenny stands up and puts his hands on the table. "Miss Farraday. I don't believe I'm hearing this."
Mandy sits back in her chair, **stunned**.
"Now. What time did you get up yesterday?" the inspector asks her.
Mandy starts playing with the buttons on her coat. "About half past six."
"Are you sure?"
"Yes."

Mit der Wendung **how come?** fragt man umgangssprachlich nach einer Erklärung. Auf Deutsch würde man sagen: *wie das?, wieso?*

"How come[i] Miss Dunbar saw you leaving the house at half past four?"
"What!"
Mandy looks away. Inspector Kenny's voice gets a little louder.
"I'm waiting, Miss Farraday?"

stunned benommen; fassungslos

"Oh, now I remember. I went to the bakery. I wanted to give daddy a nice surprise."
"Which bakery?" the inspector asks sharply.
"Bennets. It's only ten minutes walk from our house."
"Well, I don't know any bakery in London that opens before 6 a.m.," the inspector says.
"That's right. They were closed, so I went home again."
"That's strange, Mandy," Inspector Kenny replies. "We arrived at your house just after seven yesterday. Miss Dunbar said you got

home ten minutes before us. So, it takes you two and a half hours to walk to the bakery and home again. Didn't you say it was only ten minutes?"

Mandy Farraday starts to panic and gets hysterical.

"Okay, okay. I went to the Starlight to confront Linda. The night before, we argued about daddy. He promised her ten thousand pounds to continue her studies in New Zealand. That's all my money!"

marriage	Ehe
to sob	schluchzen
ϟ to lose it	ausrasten, die Beherrschung verlieren
to bash	heftig schlagen
on the charge of murder	wegen Mordverdachts

"I would say it's your father's money," Inspector Kenny replies calmly. "Did you see Linda at the disco?"

"Yes. She was just coming out of the door. She said that Ned knew about the baby and that she would marry him."

"So you followed her to the park?"

"Yes. I was in a rage," Mandy explains while she is still playing with the buttons. "I knew she was meeting Ned there and I wanted to speak to him. To tell him not to marry her."

"Ned didn't come, right?"

"Right. I was hiding in some bushes behind the bench. I remember thinking: she gets everything. A handsome man, a baby, marriage and my ten thousand pounds."

"So what did you do?"

"While I was waiting there, a jogger ran past," Mandy sobs. "I... I saw Linda give him her flirty smile and I... I just lost it. I... I saw red. There was a heavy branch on the ground, I picked it up and bashed her on the back of the head," Mandy says, tears running down her face.

Inspector Robert Kenny stands up. "Miss Mandy Farraday, I'm arresting you on the charge of murder."

Exercise 13: Translation. Übersetzen Sie die Aussagen ins Englische!

1. Ned Taylor besitzt eine Disco.

   ____

2. Linda wollte ihr Studium fortsetzen.

   ____

3. Mandy ist ein sehr eifersüchtiges Mädchen.

   ____

4. Dr. Farraday ist ein sehr konservativer Mann.

   ____

5. Es gibt drei oder vier Verdächtige.

   ____

6. Inspector Kenny hat Hochzeitstag.

   ____

Final Test

Answers

Glossary

List of Exercises

Final Test

Exercise 1: Contracted forms. Bilden Sie die verneinte Kurzform!

1. I can __________________
2. I will __________________
3. I do __________________
4. you are __________________
5. we could __________________
6. it is __________________
7. he should __________________

Exercise 2: Fill in the blanks. Vervollständigen Sie die folgenden Aussagen zu „Terminus Waterloo Bridge"!

1. Marco hides from the police in a safe __________________.
2. Ali drives a white __________________.
3. Roberta's title is __________________.
4. Hadley's firm renovated Waterloo __________________.
5. Mr and Mrs Ibrahim have two small __________________.
6. Marco strangles the newsagent with __________________.

Exercise 3: Verb forms. Wie heißt das Präsens der folgenden Verben?

1. felt	______	7. went	______
2. tried	______	8. could	______
3. began	______	9. spoke	______
4. sat	______	10. saw	______
5. fell	______	11. froze	______
6. put	______	12. overheard	______

Exercise 4: Multiple choice. Welcher Satz enthält die richtige Übersetzung?

1. Was meinst du?
   a) ❐ What did you mean?
   b) ❐ What do you think?

2. Ich bin auf den Weg ins Polizeirevier.
   a) ❐ I am on the way to the police station.
   b) ❐ I am going in the police station.

3. Offensichtlich kannten sie die Frau.
   a) ❐ They obviously knew about the woman.
   b) ❐ They obviously knew the woman.

4. Die Frau fing an zu schreien.
   a) ❐ The woman started to shout.
   b) ❐ The woman started to cry.

Exercise 5: Match up the phrases. Bilden Sie sinnvolle Wendungen!

1. ☐ arrest — a) a game
2. ☐ do — b) for back-up
3. ☐ drive — c) a post-mortem examination
4. ☐ call — d) a motorbike
5. ☐ find — e) a criminal
6. ☐ ride — f) a clue
7. ☐ play — g) a car

Exercise 6: Verb forms. Vervollständigen Sie die Sätze mit den korrekten Verbformen!

1. Frank and Barry (be) ______________ two detectives.
2. Mrs Hutchinson (invite) ______________ the detectives to tea last Thursday.
3. The mayor (like, wear) ______________ elegant clothes.
4. Mr Monks (lose) ______________ his job because he (give) ______________ bank secrets to the investment experts.
5. Yesterday, Constable Jones (find) ______________ the body in the house.
6. The supermarket (open) ______________ every day at 9 a.m.

Exercise 7: Questions about the text. Beantworten Sie die folgenden Fragen zu „Murder in Battersea Park"!

1. Who saw Mandy leave the house very early?

___

2. Who has a surgery in Harley Street?

___

3. What was the man who found the body in the park doing?

___

4. What kind of studies did Linda want to continue?

___

5. How far is the bakery from the Farraday house?

___

6. Where does Sandra Williams work?

___

Exercise 8: Unscramble the words. Bringen Sie die Buchstaben in die richtige Reihenfolge!

1. sassisan ___
2. yarom ___
3. drewi ___
4. wronf ___
5. leckuch ___
6. lameef ___
7. suttr ___

Exercise 9: Translation quiz. Übersetzen Sie und enträtseln Sie das Lösungswort!

1. blass □ _ _
2. hupen _ □ _ _
3. tragisch _ _ _ _ □ _
4. streicheln □ _ _ _ _ _
5. einsam _ □ _ _ _ _
6. Krebs (Krankheit) _ _ □ _ _ _

Lösung: □□□□□□

Answers

Terminus Waterloo Bridge

Exercise 1: **1.** a **2.** b **3.** a **4.** b **5.** b

Exercise 2: **1.** sea **2.** trousers **3.** childs **4.** feet **5.** slim **6.** motorbike

Exercise 3:
1. I want to speak to Inspector Fletcher.
2. You aren't very polite.
3. Good morning, can I help you?
4. Why are you so nervous?
5. Ali gets out of the car.
6. He walks to the shop door and unlocks it.

Exercise 4: **1.** false **2.** true **3.** true **4.** false **5.** false **6.** false

Exercise 5: **1.** outside **2.** in **3.** down **4.** walk **5.** old **6.** death **7.** men **8.** white **9.** good

Exercise 6: **1.** c **2.** b **3.** c **4.** a **5.** b **6.** a

Exercise 7:
1. I have an idea.
2. The computer produces five names.
3. Mrs Ibrahim answers the door.
4. Jack and Roberta enter the house.
5. Police cars are now arriving at the shop.

Exercise 8: **1.** red **2.** yellow **3.** blue **4.** green **5.** brown **6.** white **7.** black

Lösung: Roberta

Exercise 9: **1.** g **2.** e **3.** f **4.** a **5.** d **6.** c **7.** b

Exercise 10: **1.** office **2.** immediately **3.** door **4.** probably **5.** shows **6.** fingerprint **7.** later

Exercise 11: **1.** Yes, Dr Bird works in the autopsy room.
2. Roberta calls the hospital to get the report of the post-mortem.
3. Clive Hadley owns a building company.
4. Roberta claps her hands because she finds out Marco's identity.
5. Jack gets Roberta a coffee.
6. Roberta calls up "method of killing".

Exercise 12: **1.** photo **2.** man **3.** sure **4.** sister **5.** win **6.** upstairs **7.** play

Exercise 13: **1.** d **2.** h **3.** f **4.** g **5.** b **6.** e **7.** c **8.** a

Exercise 14: **1.** from **2.** fastest **3.** begun **4.** running **5.** bridge **6.** jumps **7.** running **8.** grins

Exercise 15: **1.** engine **2.** bodyguard **3.** million **4.** motorbike **5.** disappear

A Nice Neighbourhood

Exercise 1: **1.** bigger, biggest **2.** more comfortable, most comfortable **3.** heavier, heaviest **4.** colder, coldest **5.** better, best **6.** slower, slowest

Exercise 2: **1.** size **2.** butcher **3.** dies **4.** posters **5.** outside

Exercise 3: **1.** Where did he use to work?
2. How did you use to get to work?
3. How did the detectives use to contact each other?
4. Where did people use to post their letters?
5. When did Mr Philips use to receive his patients in the village hall?

Exercise 4: **1.** true **2.** false **3.** false **4.** true **5.** true

Exercise 5: **1.** chaotic **2.** full **3.** football **4.** house **5.** meal **6.** thief

Exercise 6: **1.** ring **2.** murderer **3.** show **4.** light **5.** papers **6.** everyone

Exercise 7: **1.** hate/dislike **2.** murder/kill **3.** mug/cup **4.** happen/take place **5.** say/remark **6.** trio/three people

Exercise 8: **1.** once **2.** husband **3.** biscuits **4.** kitchen **5.** table **6.** lonely **7.** friends

Exercise 9: **1.** poison **2.** mayor **3.** lives **4.** wearing **5.** papers **6.** twitch

Exercise 10: **1.** The mayor comes out to greet them.
2. His wrinkles show deep frustration.
3. Detective Durham does not like the mayor very much.
4. The detective finds warfarin in Miss Chambers's kitchen.
5. They managed to bankrupt whole families.

Exercise 11: **1.** tell **2.** steal **3.** begin **4.** think **5.** know **6.** can

Exercise 12: **1.** doesn't he **2.** isn't he **3.** doesn't he **4.** didn't he **5.** won't he **6.** wouldn't it

Exercise 13: **1.** a **2.** b **3.** b **4.** b

Murder in Battersea Park

Exercise 1: **1.** jogging **2.** bench **3.** handbag **4.** pulse **5.** snore **6.** shower **7.** anniversary

Exercise 2: **1.** home **2.** protect **3.** swim **4.** young **5.** bench **6.** clothes **7.** dog

Exercise 3: **1.** daughter **2.** cup **3.** apologize **4.** night **5.** seem

Exercise 4: **1.** empty **2.** woman **3.** open **4.** show **5.** ask

Exercise 5: **1.** Mr Taylor was at home at 6 a.m. this morning.
2. Inspector Kenny's assistant is called Sergeant Kelly North.

3. The name of the murdered girl is Linda Farraday.
4. Mr Taylor's disco is called Starlight.
5. Mr Taylor wears a silver stud in his left ear.

Exercise 6: **1.** brought (bring) **2.** inter view (interview) **3.** wen (when) **4.** baad (bad) **5.** playt (played) **6.** come (comes) **7.** thems (them) **8.** kup (cup) **9.** Fery (Very) **10.** ani (any)

Exercise 7: **1.** d **2.** g **3.** f **4.** b **5.** e **6.** a **7.** c

Exercise 8: **1.** I am not the murderer.
2. I saw a woman walking a dog.
3. She was expecting my child.
4. What can his motive be?
5. It all seems too easy.

Exercise 9: **1.** in **2.** in **3.** on **4.** at **5.** at **6.** At, in

Exercise 10: **1.** safe **2.** speak **3.** really **4.** girl **5.** later **6.** decide **7.** leave **8.** yesterday

Lösung: Farraday

Exercise 11: **1.** b **2.** a **3.** b **4.** c **5.** c

Exercise 12: **1.** d **2.** g **3.** e **4.** b **5.** f **6.** a **7.**c

Exercise 13: **1.** Ned Taylor owns a disco.
2. Linda wanted to continue her studies.
3. Mandy is a very jealous girl.
4. Dr Farraday is a very conservative man.
5. There are three or four suspects.
6. It is Inspector Kenny's wedding anniversary.

Final Test

Exercise 1: **1.** I can't **2.** I won't **3.** I don't **4.** you aren't **5.** we couldn't **6.** it isn't **7.** he shouldn't

Exercise 2: **1.** house **2.** Golf **3.** Inspector **4.** Bridge **5.** children **6.** piano wire

Exercise 3: **1.** feel **2.** try **3.** begin **4.** sit **5.** fall **6.** put **7.** go **8.** can **9.** speak **10.** see **11.** freeze **12.** overhear

Exercise 4: **1.** b **2.** a **3.** b **4.** a

Exercise 5: **1.** e **2.** c **3.** g **4.** b **5.** f **6.** d **7.** a

Exercise 6: **1.** are **2.** invited **3.** likes to wear/wearing **4.** lost, gave **5.** found **6.** opens

Exercise 7: **1.** Miss Dunbar saw Mandy leave the house very early.
2. Dr Farraday has a surgery in Harley Street.
3. The man who found the body in the park was jogging.
4. Linda wanted to continue her medical studies.
5. The bakery is a ten minutes' walk from the Farraday house.
6. Sandra Williams works at the Starlight Disco.

Exercise 8: **1.** assassin **2.** mayor **3.** weird **4.** frown **5.** chuckle **6.** female **7.** trust

Exercise 9: **1.** pale **2.** honk **3.** tragic **4.** stroke **5.** lonely **6.** cancer
Lösung: poison

Glossary

ϟ = umgangssprachlich

pl = Plural

abuse	Beschimpfung(en); Missbrauch
according to	laut, zufolge
to accuse sb. of sth.	jmd. etw. vorwerfen
to adopt	adoptieren
amazement	Erstaunen
ammunition	Munition
amusement	Vergnügung, Unterhaltung
annoyed	verärgert
annual	jährlich
application	Bewerbung
to appreciate sth.	etw. zu schätzen wissen
to approach	sich nähern
argument	Auseinandersetzung, Streit; Argument
armed	bewaffnet
arms dealer	Waffenhändler(in)
to arrest	verhaften

assassin	Auftragsmörder(in), Attentäter(in)
assassination	Ermordung, Attentat
assistance	Hilfe, Unterstützung
to assume	vermuten, annehmen
at full speed	mit voller Geschwindigkeit
at such short notice	so kurzfristig
available	verfügbar; erhältlich
awful	furchtbar, schrecklich
to back off	zurückgehen, zurückweichen
back-up	Verstärkung
bad feeling	*hier*: böses Blut
badge	Abzeichen
bad-tempered	schlecht gelaunt
to bang	knallen, poltern
to bankrupt	(finanziell) ruinieren
to bash	heftig schlagen
to be a handful	schwierig sein
to be (fast) asleep	(tief und fest) schlafen
bell	Klingel, Glocke
to be miles away	mit den Gedanken ganz woanders sein
bend	Kurve
to be on one's own	auf sich allein gestellt sein
besides	außerdem
to bet (bet, bet)	wetten
to be terrified	panische Angst haben
to be up to no good	nichts Gutes im Schilde führen

to blame sb. (for sth.)	jmd. beschuldigen, jmd. die Schuld an etw. geben; jmd. etw. verübeln
bless him	*hier*: die gute Seele
blow	Schlag
to blush	rot werden, erröten
body	Leiche; Körper
bookshelves *pl*	Bücherregale
to bother sb.	jmd. belästigen; jmd. beschäftigen
bright(ly)	*hier*: freudig, fröhlich; hell
to burst into tears	in Tränen ausbrechen
cancer	Krebs (Krankheit)
capable of	fähig, in der Lage zu
cardigan	Strickjacke
carnation	Nelke
case	Fall; Koffer
to catch fire	Feuer fangen
to catch one's breath	den Atem anhalten
to cause	verursachen
cause of death	Todesursache
centre of attention	Zentrum der Aufmerksamkeit
to change the subject	das Thema wechseln
to cheat (on sb.)	(jmd.) betrügen
Chippendale (furniture)	teure Möbelmarke aus dem 18. Jahrhundert
choking noises *pl*	Würgegeräusche
to chuckle	kichern, glucksen
churchgoer	Kirchgänger(in)

church hall	Gemeindehalle
to clap	klatschen
to clear sth. up	etw. (auf)klären
close-knit community	enge Gemeinschaft
clue	Hinweis, Spur
coincidence	Zufall
ϟ to come down a bit	ϟ (wieder) runterkommen
to comment	(etw.) kommentieren
commission	*hier*: Provision; Kommission
common	häufig, (weit) verbreitet
to confess	gestehen; beichten
to confirm	bestätigen
confirmation	Bestätigung
confirmed bachelor	überzeugter Junggeselle
confused	verwirrt
constable	Polizist(in), Wachtmeister
contract	Vertrag
counter	Tresen, Theke
to crawl	kriechen
to creak	knarren; quietschen
to creep (crept, crept)	schleichen, kriechen
to cremate	einäschern
crime scene	Tatort
criminal record	Vorstrafe; Vorstrafenregister
crumb	Brösel
curious	neugierig
to curse	fluchen
ϟ damn	ϟ verdammt, verflucht

to dare (to)	(etw.) wagen
dazed	benommen
dead end	Sackgasse
deadliness	Tödlichkeit
death certificate	Sterbeurkunde
to dehydrate	austrocknen, Wasser entziehen
delighted	erfreut, entzückt
demanding	fordernd, anspruchsvoll
to depend on	abhängen von
to dial	wählen (Telefon)
dickie bow	Fliege (Krawatte)
digestion	Verdauung
direction	Richtung
dirty look	böser Blick
disadvantage	Nachteil
disgust	Ekel
disgusting	ekelhaft, abstoßend
to dissolve	(sich) auflösen, verflüssigen
to distract	ablenken
to disturb	durcheinanderbringen; stören
dizzy	schwindlig
to do sb. a favour	jmd. einen Gefallen tun
docks *pl*	Hafen(anlage)
Don't mention it!	Keine Ursache!, Nicht der Rede wert!
dose	Dosis
duty sergeant	diensthabende(r) Polizist(in)
easy pickings *pl*	leichte Beute

Egyptian mummy	ägyptische Mumie
elderly	ältere(r), ältlich
embarrassed	verlegen
emergency service	Notdienst
engaged	verlobt; besetzt
engine	Motor
enormous	riesig, enorm
entrance	Eingang, Zugang
envelope	Briefumschlag
escort	Eskorte, Geleitschutz
estate car	Kombiwagen
evidence	Beweis(e)
to exclaim	(aus)rufen
expression	(Gesichts-)Ausdruck
fair enough	in Ordnung
↯ to fancy sb.	↯ auf jmd. stehen
female	weiblich
file	Akte; Datei
↯ to fire sb.	↯ jmd. feuern
to flash	(auf)blinken, blitzen, funkeln
for a change	zur Abwechslung
for dear life	um des nackten Lebens willen
forehead	Stirn
forensics	Spurensicherung
for the record	für das Protokoll
fortune	Vermögen; Schicksal
to frown	die Stirn runzeln
to fumble	herumtasten

gadget	Gerät, technische Spielerei
to gasp	keuchen, nach Luft schnappen
general practitioner	Allgemeinmediziner, Hausarzt
gentle, gently	sanft, zärtlich
to get (straight) down to business	(gleich) zur Sache kommen
to get one's skates on	↯ ein bisschen dalli machen
to get on (with sb.)	(mit jmd.) auskommen
to get (straight) to the point	(gleich) auf den Punkt kommen
to glance (at)	schauen (auf)
glove compartment	Handschuhfach
gossip	Tratsch, Klatsch
to grab	packen, greifen
graveyard	Friedhof
greasy	fettig
to grimace	das Gesicht verziehen
grim(ly)	grimmig, streng
groan	Stöhnen
guilty conscience	schlechtes Gewissen
gut feeling	Bauchgefühl
handcuffs *pl*	Handschellen
handle	Griff; (Tür-)Klinke
handrail	Handlauf
hatred	Hass
headline	Schlagzeile
headscarf	Kopftuch
to hesitate	zögern

hit	*hier*: Treffer
to honk	hupen
horse breeder	Pferdezüchter(in)
housekeeper	Haushälterin
House of Commons	britisches Unterhaus
How dare you!	Wie können Sie es wagen!
to hug sb.	jmd. umarmen
to humour sb.	jmd. seinen Willen lassen
hunch	(Vor-)Ahnung, Intuition
identity card	(Dienst-)Ausweis
I'm afraid (not)	leider (nicht)
imaginary	imaginär, eingebildet
impatient(ly)	ungeduldig
in charge (of)	zuständig (für); leiten
in defeat	niedergeschlagen
ingredient	Zutat; Bestandteil
insider trading	Insiderhandel (mit Aktien)
to insist	beharren, bestehen auf
insurance	Versicherung
to intend	beabsichtigen
intently	intensiv, durchdringend
to interrogate	verhören, befragen
investigation	Ermittlung, Untersuchung
investigator	Ermittler(in)
to involve	beteiligen; betreffen
irritably	gereizt
jealous (of)	eifersüchtig (auf), neidisch (auf)
to jerk	zucken

to jump	erschrecken, zusammenzucken; springen
kind	Art, Sorte
kitchenette	Kochnische
to kneel (knelt, knelt) down	sich hinknien
late shift	Spätschicht
let me handle this	lass/lassen Sie mich das in die Hand nehmen
to look forward to	sich freuen auf
↯ to lose (lost, lost) it	ausrasten, die Beherrschung verlieren
lounge	Wohnzimmer; Gesellschaftsraum
madness	Wahnsinn
magistrate	Amtsrichter(in)
make	Marke, Fabrikat
to make a big deal of sth.	viel Wind um etw. machen
malpractice	Berufsvergehen; Amtsmissbrauch
manners *pl*	Manieren, Benehmen
marriage	Ehe
to match	passen zu; vergleichen
matter	Sache, Angelegenheit
mayor	Bürgermeister(in)
meanwhile	inzwischen, unterdessen
medical studies	Medizinstudium
menacing	bedrohlich
mercy	Erbarmen, Gnade

to mess sb. about	jmd. an der Nase herumführen
middle-aged	mittleren Alters
↯ minx	↯ freches Ding, Zicke
morgue	Leichenschauhaus
mounted on	montiert auf
to mumble	murmeln, nuscheln
murder	Mord
to murder	(er)morden
to mutter	(vor sich hin)murmeln, brummeln
nameplate	Namensschild
napkin	Serviette
nasty	scheußlich; böse; gehässig
neat	ordentlich, sauber
to need stitches	genäht werden müssen
nephew	Neffe
newsagent	Zeitungshändler, Zeitschriftenladen
the night before last	vorgestern Abend
to nod	nicken
no matches	keine Treffer
nothing ... but	nichts als, nur
nowadays	heutzutage
objection	Einwand, Einspruch
to observe	feststellen, beobachten
obsessed	besessen
obvious(ly)	offensichtlich
Oh dear!	Meine Güte!; Oje!
old-fashioned	altmodisch
old maid	alte Jungfer

on the charge of murder	wegen Mordverdachts
to overhear (-heard, -heard)	zufällig (mit)hören
pale	blass, bleich
to pat	*hier*: (Haare) zurechtstreichen; tätscheln
pathologist	Gerichtsmediziner(in)
payment	(Be-)Zahlung
pedestrian	Fußgänger(in)
piano wire	Klavierdraht
pigsty	Schweinestall
pile	Stapel, Haufen
to pinch	zwicken
pin-striped suit	Nadelstreifenanzug
plump	mollig, pummelig
poison	Gift
post-mortem (examination)	Obduktion
to pour sb. sth.	jmd. etw. einschenken
prayer	Gebet
pregnant	schwanger
presence	Anwesenheit, Gegenwart
to presume	vermuten, annehmen
to pretend	vorgeben, vortäuschen
prison	Gefängnis
prisoner	Gefangene(r)
proof	Beweis(e)
proper	ordentlich; passend

property	Immobilien; Eigentum; Eigenschaft
to protect	(be)schützen
proud	stolz
to prove (proved, proven)	beweisen
to put (sb.) through	(jmd.) durchstellen, verbinden (Telefon)
puzzled	verblüfft, verwirrt
to question sb.	jmd. befragen
rage	Wut(anfall); Zorn
to raise sb.	jmd. großziehen; jmd. wecken
rearview mirror	Rückspiegel
to receive	erhalten, empfangen
receiver	Telefonhörer; Empfänger
recently	kürzlich, jüngst
recognition signal	Erkennungszeichen
registration number	polizeiliches Kennzeichen
to release	freigeben, freilassen
to relive sth.	etw. nochmals durchleben
remains *pl*	Überreste
to remind sb. (of sth.)	jmd. (an etw.) erinnern
to report	melden, berichten; anzeigen
to research	(er)forschen
research	Recherche; Forschung
to rest	(aus)ruhen
revenge	Rache
rewind button	Rückspultaste
rifle	Gewehr

rigor mortis	Leichenstarre
rocket	Rakete
to rush	eilen
safe house	sicherer Unterschlupf
safety belt	Sicherheitsgurt
to save one's own skin	seine eigene Haut retten
savings *pl*	Ersparnisse
to scratch	kratzen
screech	Quietschen, Kreischen
search warrant	Durchsuchungsbefehl
self-important	selbstgefällig
to sense	spüren, fühlen
serious	ernst
Serves them right!	Das geschieht ihnen recht!
to settle sth.	etw. regeln
severe	heftig; streng
shame	Schande; Scham
shiver	Schauer; Zittern
to show sb. in(to)	jmd. hereinführen
to shrug (one's shoulders)	die Achseln zucken
to sigh	seufzen
sigh (of relief)	Seufzer (der Erleichterung)
signature	Unterschrift
to sign	unterzeichnen
signed	unterschrieben
to sip	nippen, trinken
sip	Schluck

to skid	schleudern, rutschen
slave	Sklave/Sklavin
slim	schlank
smart	schick; schlau
smashed	zertrümmert
to sneer	spöttisch lächeln
to sniff	schniefen
to snore	schnarchen
to snort	schnauben, prusten
to sob	schluchzen
to solve	lösen; aufklären
spare key	Ersatzschlüssel
speed trap	Radarfalle
spine	Rückgrat
ϟ spinster	(alte) Jungfer
to spread (spread, spread)	(sich) verbreiten
to squeeze	drücken
St Peter's gates *pl*	Himmelspforte
to stare	starren
to starve	(ver)hungern
to state	angeben; feststellen
steering wheel	Lenkrad
sticky	klebrig
stiff	steif
to stir (sth.)	(etw.) (um)rühren
stockbroker	Aktienhändler(in), Börsenmakler(in)
storeroom	Lagerraum

strangled	erwürgt
stream	Bach
strength	Kraft, Stärke
to stroke	streicheln, streichen über
stud	(Ohr-)Stecker
to stumble	stolpern
stunned	benommen; fassungslos
stupidity	Dummheit
to sulk	schmollen
superior	Vorgesetzte(r)
to support	(unter)stützen
to suppose	annehmen, vermuten
surgery	*hier*: Arztpraxis; Chirurgie
suspected	mutmaßlich; tatverdächtig
suspicion	Verdacht
suspicious	verdächtig; misstrauisch
to swallow	schlucken
sweat	Schweiß
switch	Schalter
to take advantage of	ausnutzen
to take aim	zielen
to take over	übernehmen, ablösen
tap	Wasserhahn
tax office	Finanzamt
terminus	Endstation
That's all for now.	Das war's fürs Erste.
theft	Diebstahl
ϟ the joke is on me	ϟ ich bin der Dumme

thoughtfully	nachdenklich; aufmerksam
to threaten	(be)drohen
tidy	ordentlich, aufgeräumt
tissue	Papiertaschentuch
to trace	aufspüren; (zurück)verfolgen
trapdoor	Falltür
tray	Tablett
to treat	behandeln
troublemaker	Unruhestifter(in)
to trust	(ver)trauen
trusting	vertrauensvoll
to tug	zupfen
to tut	sich mokieren
tweed	Wollstoff, Tweed
twitch	Zucken, Zuckung
unbearable	unerträglich
unconscious	bewusstlos
undertaker	Bestatter(in)
uneducated	ungebildet
upset	aufgeregt, verärgert
used to be	(mal) gewesen sein
used to do sth.	etw. (früher) getan haben
victim	Opfer
villager	Dorfbewohner(in)
wallet	Brieftasche
wardrobe	Kleiderschrank
to wash one's dirty linen in public	seine schmutzige Wäsche in der Öffentlichkeit waschen

to waste	verschwenden
to wave (one's hands)	winken; schwenken
wedding anniversary	Hochzeitstag
weird	seltsam; unheimlich
whine	Gejammer
to whisper	flüstern
whisper	Flüstern
to whistle	pfeifen
will	Testament; Wille
winding	(sich) biegend, windend
to wink	zwinkern
to wipe	(ab)wischen
to wipe out	auslöschen
witness	Zeuge/Zeugin
wrinkle	Falte, Fältchen
X-ray	Röntgenbild
yard	Längenmaß: 91 cm
zebra crossing	Zebrastreifen

List of Exercises

Lernkrimi Lektüren Englisch

A1

A Cry in the Darkness
Kurzkrimis
ISBN 978-3-8174-9984-7

Deadly Thanksgiving
Kurzkrimis
ISBN 978-3-8174-1756-8

Death at Land's End
Kurzkrimis
ISBN 978-3-8174-9658-7

The Murderer Next Door
Kurzkrimis
ISBN 978-3-8174-9438-5

A2

Blood and Breakfast
Kurzkrimis
ISBN 978-3-8174-1385-0

Deadly Business
Kurzkrimis
ISBN 978-3-8174-9215-2

Last Exit Waterloo Bridge
Kurzkrimis
ISBN 978-3-8174-1863-3

Murder at Teatime
Kurzkrimis
ISBN 978-3-8174-1856-5

Learning by Killing
Kurzkrimis
ISBN 978-3-8174-1388-1

Long Time No Kill
Classic
ISBN 978-3-8174-9794-2

Murderous Collection
Sammelband 10 in 1
ISBN 978-3-8174-8967-1

B1

Bullets over Bristol
Kurzkrimis
ISBN 978-3-8174-8544-4

Death Comes Knocking
Kurzkrimis
ISBN 978-3-8174-7945-0

Murderous Network
Kurzkrimis
ISBN 978-3-8174-9312-8

Art and Ashes
Classic
ISBN 978-3-8174-9493-4

Cook and Kill
Classic
ISBN 978-3-8174-9492-7

Deadly Mistake
Classic
ISBN 978-3-8174-8259-7

Death Wasn't the Deal
Classic
ISBN 978-3-8174-9491-0

London Crime Time
Sammelband 3 in 1
ISBN 978-3-8174-7787-6

Bone by Bone
Lernthriller
ISBN 978-3-8174-9497-2

Faceless Killer
Lernthriller
ISBN 978-3-8174-8856-8

Massacre United
Lernthriller
ISBN 978-3-8174-9319-7

Lernkrimi Lektüren Englisch

B2

Bloody Diamonds
Classic
ISBN 978-3-8174-9494-1

Nobody Dies Twice
Classic
ISBN 978-3-8174-9495-8

In Terror
Lernthriller
ISBN 978-3-8174-8857-5

C1

A Scottish Murder Mystery
Classic
ISBN 978-3-8174-8379-2

Keep Calm and Carry On Killing
Classic
ISBN 978-3-8174-1644-8

Lernkrimi Comic Englisch

A1

Chasing Bloody Mary
ISBN 978-3-8174-1655-4

Lernkrimi Sprachkurs Englisch

A1/A2

Lernkrimi Sprachkurs
ISBN 978-3-8174-7844-5

Lernkrimi Hörbücher Englisch

Black Wedding
ISBN 978-3-8174-1817-6

Dangerous Deals
ISBN 978-3-8174-9988-5

A Shot in the Night
ISBN 978-3-8174-8202-3

The Butterworth Mystery
ISBN 978-3-8174-8203-0

Death Wish
ISBN 978-3-8174-8204-7

Strangled
ISBN 978-3-8174-1876-3

Bloody Revenge
ISBN 978-3-8174-8860-5

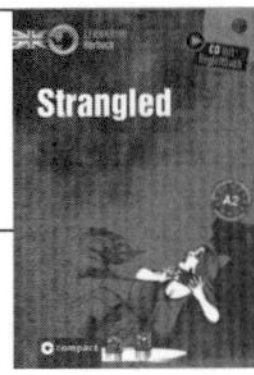

Bloody Legacy
ISBN 978-3-8174-7676-3

Crime & Company
ISBN 978-3-8174-8976-3

Murder at the Office
ISBN 978-3-8174-7747-0

Lernkrimi Rätselblöcke Englisch

A1
Murderous Games
ISBN 978-3-8174-9500-9

A2
The Art of Crime
ISBN 978-3-8174-9155-1

B1
A Deadly Puzzle
ISBN 978-3-8174-8832-2